The Tw~~ight of Equality?~~

The Twilight of Equality?

Neoliberalism, Cultural Politics, and the Attack on Democracy

Lisa Duggan

Beacon Press, Boston

BEACON PRESS
25 Beacon Street
Boston, Massachusetts 02108-2892
www.beacon.org

Beacon Press books
are published under the auspices of
the Unitarian Universalist Association of Congregations.

12 11 10 09   8 7 6 5 4 3

This book is printed on acid-free paper that meets the uncoated paper
ANSI/NISO specifications for permanence as revised in 1992.

Text design by Isaac Tobin
Composition by Wilsted & Taylor Publishing Services

Library of Congress Cataloging-in-Publication Data
Duggan, Lisa
    Neoliberalism, cultural politics, and the attack on democracy / Lisa Duggan. —1st ed.
        p. cm.
Includes bibliographical references and index.

    ISBN 978-0-8070-7955-3 (pbk.)
    1. Liberalism—United States. 2. Democracy—United States. I. Title.
JC574.2.U6D84 2003
320.51′3′0973—dc21   2003010442

FOR HENRY ABELOVE AND CINDY PATTON

Contents

Introduction

What a long, strange trip it's been.

When I graduated from high school in 1972, the United States did not appear to be in good condition. Richard Nixon was president, the U.S. was embroiled in an unjust imperialist war in Vietnam, the limitations of 1960s civil rights legislation appeared in the form of persistent, entrenched racial inequality, the worlds of work and home were sharply segmented by gender hierarchies. But in 1972, I nonetheless had reason to be optimistic. Active and expanding social movements seemed capable of ameliorating conditions of injustice and inequality, poverty, war and imperialism. In fact, social movements were producing innovative critiques of a widening variety of constraints on human possibility—the women's liberation movement, gay liberation, lesbian feminism, black feminism, and other thriving or emerging formations joined radical labor activism, civil rights and black nationalist insurgencies, antiracist and anti-imperialist mobilizations. Despite all the internal tensions and conflicts, it also seemed possible that cross-fertilizations would incite exponential growth in the scope and impact of our shared or overlapping visions of social change. When I said I wanted to be a "revolutionary," this was not received as ludicrous or sectarian, but as a declaration of affinity with those whose overlapping aspirations for equality—social, political, economic, and cultural equality in a global context—seemed both thrilling and attainable.

I had no idea I was not perched at a great beginning, but rather at a denouement, as the possibilities for progressive social change encountered daunting historical setbacks beginning in 1972. From the perspective of more than three decades later, it is apparent that a great sea change begun in the early 1970s led us all in directions we simply could not have imagined then. From the early 1970s, global competition and falling profit rates stirred U.S. corporate interests to mount a counter-movement. This movement expanded in many directions from its base of pro-business activism, and it took many years to build; it has never been unified or stable. Yet, it has successfully opposed proliferating visions of an expansive, more equitable redistribution of the world's resources. Beginning with the election of Ronald Reagan to the presidency and throughout the 1980s, the overall direction of redistribution of many kinds of resources, in the U.S. and around the world, has been upward—toward greater concentration among fewer hands at the very top of an increasingly steep pyramid.

What happened? How did the forces of upward redistribution so forcefully trump the broad-based, expansive "revolution" toward downward redistributions that seemed so vital still in 1972? In the United States, the uneasy and uneven New Deal consensus among business, government, and big unions, built during the 1930s and more or less in place through the Great Society era of the 1960s, was dismantled. But this did not occur in order to remedy the undemocratic and antiegalitarian features of that consensus, or in order to generate greater democratic participation, material equality, cultural diversity, and good global citizenship, as many "revolutionaries" had hoped. Rather, the New Deal consensus was dismantled in the creation of a new vision of national and world order, a vision of competition, inequality, market "discipline," public austerity, and "law and order" known as *neoliberalism*.[1]

Tracing their descent through capital "L" Liberalism, as developed in Anglo-Europe since the seventeenth century, the architects of contemporary neoliberalism drew upon classical liberalism's utopianism of benevolent "free" markets and minimal governments. These earlier ideas provided a set of rationales, moral justifications, and politically inflected descriptions of the institutions of developing capitalism. Such institutions, and their associated economic practices and social relations, changed over time and varied across space—capitalism has never been a single coherent "system." Liberalism has therefore morphed many times as well, and has contained proliferating contradictions in

indirect relationship to the historic   ʲtalism. In
the United States during the twentieth   ˋ of
mainstream electoral politics, from "conserva   ⌐
alism," has varied largely within the parameters of Libɛ……
far right and the left have provided illiberal or antiliberal alternatɪ……
the overwhelming dominance of differing and conflicting forms of Liberalism in U.S. politics.[2]

From the 1930s to the 1960s, a very limited form of welfare state liberalism, or social democracy, shaped the U.S. nation state and the political culture supporting it. The New Deal coalition defeated or marginalized antistatist conservatives (who were also Liberals in the classical sense), and absorbed or marginalized socialists and other progressive left critics of its limited version of equality within capitalism. During the 1950s and 1960s, criticism of the U.S. welfare state from both the right and the left intensified. Conservative antistatist attacks on New Deal social welfare programs mounted, as the new social movements pressed from the left for more equitable distribution of many kinds of resources. Then during the 1970s, the social movements encountered a new pro-business activism that ultimately seized the primary institutions of the state over the next two decades.

This pro-business activism, the foundation for late twentieth century neoliberalism, was built out of earlier "conservative" activism. Neoliberalism developed over many decades as a mode of polemic aimed at dismantling the limited U.S. welfare state, in order to enhance corporate profit rates. The raising of profit rates required that money be diverted from other social uses, thus increasing overall economic inequality. And such diversions required a supporting political culture, compliant constituencies, and amenable social relations. Thus, pro-business activism in the 1970s was built on, and further developed, a wide-ranging political and cultural project—the reconstruction of the everyday life of capitalism, in ways supportive of upward redistribution of a range of resources, and tolerant of widening inequalities of many kinds.[3]

Neoliberalism developed primarily in the U.S., and secondarily in

Europe, in response to global changes that challenged the dominance of Western institutions. Within the U.S. specifically, one might divide the construction of neoliberal hegemony up into five phases: (1) attacks on the New Deal coalition, on progressive unionism, and on popular front political culture and progressive redistributive internationalism during the 1950s and 1960s; (2) attacks on downwardly redistributive social movements, especially the Civil Rights and Black Power movements, but including feminism, lesbian and gay liberation, and countercultural mobilizations during the 1960s and 1970s; (3) pro-business activism during the 1970s, as U.S.-based corporations faced global competition and falling profit rates, previously conflicting big and small business interests increasingly converged, and business groups organized to re-distribute resources *upward*; (4) domestically focused "culture wars" attacks on public institutions and spaces for democratic public life, in alliances with religious moralists and racial nationalists, during the 1980s and 1990s; and (5) emergent "multicultural," neoliberal "equality" politics—a stripped-down, nonredistributive form of "equality" de-signed for global consumption during the twenty-first century, and compatible with continued upward redistribution of resources.

During every phase, the construction of neoliberal politics and pol-icy in the U.S. has relied on identity and cultural politics. The politics of race, both overt and covert, have been particularly central to the en-tire project. But the politics of gender and sexuality have intersected with race and class politics at each stage as well.

Though built over several decades beginning in the 1940s and 1950s, neoliberalism *per se* is generally associated with the set of policy imper-atives for international government and business operations called the "Washington Consensus" of the 1980s and 1990s. Generated by the In-ternational Monetary Fund, the World Bank and the U.S. Treasury, and also implemented through the World Trade Organization, neoliberal policies of fiscal austerity, privatization, market liberalization, and gov-ernmental stabilization are pro-corporate capitalist guarantors of pri-vate property relations. They were designed to recreate the globe in the interests of the unimpeded operation of capitalist "free" markets, and to cut back public, noncommercial powers and resources that might impede or drain potential profit making. Nominally pro-democratic, the neoliberal financial institutions have operated autocratically themselves, primarily through financial coercion. They have also consistently supported autocratic governments and plutocratic elites around the world to promote one kind of stability—a stability designed to facilitate business investment. The effects of neoliberal policy implementation have consistently included many kinds of instability, however, including unrest associated with dramatically increasing inequality, and political fragility resulting from reduced sovereignty for national governments.

The Washington Consensus was a kind of backroom deal among the financial, business, and political elites based in the United States and Europe. Its policies reinvented practices of economic, political, and cultural imperialism for a supposedly postimperial world. Neoliberalism's avatars have presented its doctrines as universally inevitable and its operations as ultimately beneficial in the long term—even for those who must suffer through poverty and chaos in the short term. In other words, neoliberalism is a kind of secular faith. Its priests were elected by no one, and are accountable only to the global elites whose interests are promoted by its policies.

But how did pro-business activists manage to deploy the levers of government at the seat of postimperial power, in Washington, D.C.? How have global politics proceeded, out of range of democratic accountability in the United States as well as in the rest of the world? This has occurred through (A) the presentation of neoliberal policies as neutral, managerial precepts for good government and efficient business operations, with the underlying capitalist power politics and cultural values obscured; (B) the opposition between U.S. domestic *conservative* versus *liberal* politics, or Republican versus Democratic policies, with the overarching salience of global neoliberalism across this entire spectrum effectively ignored; (C) the shape-shifting array of alliances and issues through which a neoliberal policy agenda has been promoted in the United States and abroad.

(A) The most successful ruse of neoliberal dominance in both global and domestic affairs is the definition of *economic* policy as primarily a matter of neutral, technical expertise. This expertise is then presented as separate from *politics* and *culture*, and not properly subject to specifically political accountability or cultural critique. Opposition to material inequality is maligned as "class warfare," while race, gender or sexual inequalities are dismissed as merely cultural, private, or trivial. This rhetorical separation of the economic from the political and cultural arenas disguises the upwardly redistributing goals of neoliberalism—its concerted efforts to concentrate power and resources in the hands of tiny elites. Once *economics* is understood as primarily a technical realm, the trickle-upward effects of neoliberal policies can be framed as due to performance rather than design, reflecting the greater merit of those reaping larger rewards.

But, despite their overt rhetoric of separation between economic policy on the one hand, and political and cultural life on the other, neoliberal politicians and policymakers have never actually separated these domains in practice. In the real world, class and racial hierarchies, gender and sexual institutions, religious and ethnic boundaries are the channels through which money, political power, cultural resources, and social organization flow. The *economy* cannot be transparently abstracted from the *state* or the *family*, from practices of racial apartheid, gender segmentation, or sexual regulation. The illusion that such categories of social life can be practically as well as analytically abstracted one from another descends from the conceptual universe of Anglo-European Liberalism, altered and adapted to the U.S. context during the early nineteenth century (see chapter 1). While reasserting this ideology of discrete spheres of social life, in practice contemporary neoliberal policies have been implemented in and through culture and politics, reinforcing or contesting relations of class, race, gender, sexuality, ethnicity, religion, or nationality. The specific issues, alliances and policies have shifted over time and across differing locales, but their overall impact has been the upward redistribution of resources and the reproduction of stark patterns of social inequality.

(B) In the United States, specifically, the neoliberal agenda of shrinking public institutions, expanding private profit-making prerogatives, and undercutting democratic practices and noncommercial cultures has changed hands from Republicans in the 1970s and 1980s, to New Democrats in the 1990s, and back to Compassionate Conservative Republicans in the new millennium. The domestic political language of two party electoral politics, a language that labels figures and initiatives as *conservative*, *moderate*, or *liberal*, has effectively obscured the stakes in policy disputes. If Ronald Reagan was a *conservative* president, with substantial support from the religious *right*, and Bill Clinton was a *liberal* president excoriated by *conservatives* and the *right*, then why do their policy initiatives look so much alike? It was Bill Clinton who pushed the North American Free Trade Agreement through against organized labor's opposition, and who presided over "the end of welfare, as we know it." The continuities from Reagan through Bush I, Clinton to Bush II—the continuities of neoliberal policy promotion— are rendered relatively invisible by the dominant political system and language. Global neoliberalism, based in but not reducible to U.S. corporate dominance, embraces a broad spectrum of U.S. domestic politics. Conflicts between conservative Republicans and liberal Democrats have been shaped largely within the terms of neoliberalism, even as nonliberal and even antiliberal forces (from the proto-fascist nationalism of Pat Buchanan to the socialist radicalism of Cornell West) have been engaged or appropriated through alliance politics as well.

But then are there no important differences between Reagan and Clinton? Was there really no basis upon which to prefer the election of Gore over Bush II? This was the claim of Ralph Nader's presidential campaign during the 2000 election, a claim that many progressives rallied around, and others found incredible. What about the Supreme Court and the fate of *Roe v. Wade*? What about civil rights, affirmative action, gay visibility? It is at this point of confusion and dispute that the progressive left in the United States finds itself stymied. The split between those who emphasize economics, wealth distribution, corporate dominance, and the sale of political office (such as the Nader campaign) and those who emphasize political and cultural equality and access (and who were frightened by both Bush and Nader's relative indifference to issues of gender, race, and sexuality during the 2000 election) has effectively undermined progressive-left activism in the United States since 1980.

(C) If neoliberalism has been the continuing foundation for pro-business activism in the U.S. since the 1970s, that activism has also engaged a shifting array of political/cultural issues and constituencies in order to gain power and legitimacy. Because (as I have argued) the economy and the interests of business can not really be abstracted from race and gender relations, from sexuality or other cleavages in the body politic, neoliberalism has assembled its projects and interests from the field of issues saturated with race, with gender, with sex, with religion, with ethnicity, and nationality. The alliances and issues have changed over time and have differed from place to place—within the U.S. and abroad (see chapters 1–3). In order to facilitate the flow of money up the economic hierarchy, neoliberal politicians have constructed complex and shifting alliances, issue by issue and location by location—always in contexts shaped by the meanings and effects of race, gender, sexuality, and other markers of difference. These alliances are not simply opportunistic, and the issues not merely epiphenomenal or secondary to the underlying reality of the more solid and real economic goals, but rather, the economic goals have been (must be) formulated *in terms of* the range of political and cultural meanings that shape the social body in a particular time and place.

The Achilles' heel in progressive-left politics since the 1980s, especially, has been a general blindness to the connections and interrelations of the economic, political, and cultural, and a failure to grasp the shifting dimensions of the alliance politics underlying neoliberal success. As neoliberals have formed and reformed their constituencies, and produced issues and languages that connect their economic goals with politics and culture in politically effective ways, progressives and leftists have tended more and more to fall into opposing camps that caricature each other while failing to clearly perceive the chameleon that eludes them.

During the 1960s and 1970s, the proliferation and expansion of progressive-left critiques and social movements constituted a fertile ground for connections—as well as for conflict and confusion. Identifying the most significant sites of inequality and injustice, and discovering the best means for attacking them, was always a contentious project. But the range of social movements—antiracist and anti-imperialist, feminist, lesbian and gay, radical labor, and environmentalist— did not generally or easily fall into camps with economics emphasized on one side, and culture on the other. Gay liberation newspapers included anti-imperialist manifestoes and analyses of the racist legal and prison system. Black feminists set out to track the interrelations of capitalism, patriarchy, and racism. There were bitter fights among contingents of activists who prioritized one or another "vector of oppression" and dismissed others—but the economics/culture split did not appear as a major and sustained divide in U.S. progressive-left politics until the 1980s.

The progressive-left social movements of the 1960s and 1970s might be conceptualized as overlapping, interrelated (if conflicted) *cultures of downward redistribution.* The differing sectors were joined by languages and concepts, practices and policies, as well as by movement institutions that combined cultural and material resources. Such cultures were mixed, neither pure nor consistently critical of all forms of inequality and injustice or unfreedom. But in their hybrid, mongrel mixtures the overall emphasis that connected the progressive-left social movements was the pressure to level hierarchies and redistribute *down*—redistribute money, political power, cultural capital, pleasure, and freedom. They were met, from the early 1970s forward, with a pro-business counter movement intent on building a *culture of upward (re)distribution.* Business and financial interests were no more unified or consistent than the social movements, but their activities forged languages and concepts, practices and policies, and founded new institutions to promote mechanisms that either shored up or established inequalities of power, rank, wealth, or cultural status.

During the 1980s, as standards of living dropped in the United States and global inequalities expanded, social movements responded to multiple constraints and pressures in part by fragmenting, in part by accommodating to the narrowing horizons of fundraising imperatives, legal constraints, and the vice grip of electoral politics. *Identity politics,* in the contemporary sense of the rights-claiming focus of balkanized groups organized to pressure the legal and electoral systems for inclusion and redress, appeared out of the field of disintegrating social movements.[4] Single-group or single-issue organizations dedicated to lobbying, litigation, legislation, or public and media education had existed earlier *as only one part* of larger, shaping social movements. As the practical wings of broad-based mobilizations, ranging from reformist to radical on a motley collection of connected issues, such organizations usually remained intimately connected to movement cultures. But during the 1980s, such organizations—known collectively as the "civil rights lobby"—began to appear as the parts that replaced the wholes. The reproductive freedom movement receded, but the National Abortion Rights Action League remained; the Civil Rights and Black Power movements disintegrated, but the NAACP persisted. Focused narrowly on U.S. domestic politics, and even more narrowly on courtroom litigation, legislative battles or electoral campaigns, large portions of the organized efforts of social movements succumbed to liberalism's paltry promise—engage the language and institutional games of established liberal contests and achieve equality.

Many if not most of those engaged within the civil rights lobbies, or the protest and pressure politics aimed at the media and marketplace, understood the limits and false promises of the "equality" on offer through liberal reform—equality disarticulated from material life and class politics, to be won by definable "minority" groups, one at a time. They engaged a politics of the possible, often with the hope of using liberalism's own languages and rules to force change beyond the boundaries of liberal equality. Like the motley, radical union movements of earlier decades, that collapsed largely into the coopting embrace of New Deal corporatism in the post–World War II era, the social movements disintegrated, leaving their liberal reformist wings as their most visible traces. Meanwhile, the more radical and transformative segments of social movements nonetheless survived, in a range of new as well as continuing organizations and campaigns and in a growing library of progressive-left intellectual and scholarly projects and publications. Occasionally, it all came together as it had in earlier times—the movement born to fight AIDS and HIV infection linked identity and civil rights politics with an encompassing vision of material and cultural equality, and drew upon the resources of activists, theorists, artists, and scientists to construct an imaginative range of political interventions during the 1980s.[5] Overall, the remnants of the 1960s and 1970s social movements, together with the identity-based organizations and civil rights establishment of the 1980s, remained cultures of downward distribution—even if in a less generally radical sense during the 1980s.

But during the 1990s, something new happened. Neoliberals in the ranks of U.S. conservative party politics began to slowly and unevenly shed the "culture wars" alliances with religious moralists, white supremacists, ultra nationalists, and other antiliberal forces that had helped guarantee their political successes during the 1980s (phase 4, above). Neoliberal New Democrats, led by Bill Clinton, included civil rights/equality politics within a framework that minimized any downwardly redistributing impulses and effects (phase 5). And some organizations within the "civil rights lobby" narrowed their focus and moved dramatically to the right, accommodating rather than opposing the global inequalities generated by neoliberalism.

Meanwhile, activists and intellectuals on the progressive-left, operating outside the terms of two party neoliberalism, fell more deeply into unproductive battles over economic versus cultural politics, identity-based vs. left universalist rhetoric, theoretical critiques vs. practical organizing campaigns (see chapter 4). Most recently, a newly insurgent antiglobalization movement, emerging into active visibility and effectiveness at the beginning of the twenty-first century, offers a space

where such divisions might be remade into productive connections—
though this remains a possibility, and not an achievement. In general,
too few on the left have noticed that as neoliberal policies continued to
shrink the spaces for public life, democratic debate, and cultural expression during the 1990s, they were doing this *through* their own versions of identity politics and cultural policies, inextricably connected to
economic goals for upward redistribution of resources.

The Twilight of Equality? is written as an analysis of the politics of
the 1990s, and as a polemic for the twenty-first century, to argue that as
long as the progressive-left represents and reproduces itself as divided
into economic vs. cultural, universal vs. identity-based, distribution vs.
recognition-oriented, local or national vs. global branches, it will defeat
itself. On one side, the identity politics camps are increasingly divorced
from any critique of global capitalism. Some organizations and groups
creep into the neoliberal fold, shedding downwardly redistributing
goals for a stripped-down equality, paradoxically imagined as compatible with persistent overall inequality. They thus sacrifice the broad
goals that might connect a new social movement strong and ambitious
enough to take on inequalities that single-issue politics only ever ame-
liorate, but never reverse. On the other side, critiques of global capitalism and neoliberalism, and left populist or universalist politics within
the U.S., attack and dismiss cultural and identity politics at their peril.
Such attacks strip them of prime sources of political creativity and new
analyses, and leave them uncomprehending before the cultural and
identity politics of the opposition. In addition, they drive constituencies seeking equality away, toward the false promises of superficial
neoliberal "multiculturalism." In other words, they help to create what
they fearfully or critically imagine.

Chapter 1 of *The Twilight of Equality?* places contemporary neoliberalism within the context of the development of Liberalism in the United
States from the early nineteenth century. This chapter outlines how the

categories of Liberalism produce false rhetorical separations between economic, political, social, cultural, and personal life that continue to resonate in contemporary politics. The chapter then examines the politics of welfare "reform" and prison expansion in order to illuminate the concrete interconnections among the economic, political, and cultural projects of neoliberalism. Chapter 2 offers a case study of the operations of neoliberalism in phase 4 of its construction in the U.S.—the now residual phase of "culture wars" alliances. This chapter traces a sex panic that began over a women's studies conference at SUNY/New Paltz in 1997 and connects the "moral" discourse there to the tax-cutting agenda of New York state corporations. This strategy of attack on public institutions is then traced to the tax revolt begun in California, organized around Proposition 13 in the early 1970s. Chapter 3 moves to another case study focused on phase 5—the emergent "multicultural" phase of neoliberal policy promotion inaugurated in the 1990s. This chapter unravels the core arguments of a group of gay writers organized through the Independent Gay Forum, focusing especially on the writing of Andrew Sullivan. The narrow and deceptive "equality" rhetoric these writers deploy in fact generates support for neoliberal politics and global inequality. Finally, Chapter 4 argues that the split between economic justice campaigns and antiglobalization politics on one side, and identity or cultural politics on the other, is a misguided and disabling disconnection for the entire progressive-left.

Overall, *The Twilight of Equality?* argues that neoliberalism has a shifting cultural politics that the progressive-left must understand in order to constitute an effective opposition. But rather than focus on neoliberalism's cultural project, sectors of the progressive-left reproduce, within their own debates, Liberalism's rhetorical separation of economic/class politics from identity/cultural politics. This separation seriously disables political analysis and activism.

If the triumph of neoliberalism brings us into the twilight of equality, this is not an irreversible fate. This new world order was invented during the 1970s and 1980s, and dominated the 1990s, but it may now be unraveling—if we are prepared to seize the moment of its faltering, to promote and ensure its downfall. Only an interconnected, analytically diverse, cross-fertilizing and expansive left can seize this moment to lead us elsewhere, to newly imagined possibilities for equality in the twenty-first century.

1

Downsizing Democracy

That corporations have taken the spotlight as latter-day English-speaking conquistadors—Magellans of technology, Cortéses of consumer goods, and Pizarros of entertainment—reflected the cosmopolitanizing of their profits, a cousinship to earlier Dutch and then British cosmopolitanizing of investment. . . .

The last two decades of the twentieth century . . . echoed the zeniths of corruption and excess—the Gilded Age and the 1920s—when the rich in the United States slipped their usual political constraints, and this trend continued into the new century. By the 1990s data showed the United States replacing Europe at the pinnacle of Western privilege and inequality. This, of course, is part of what made the United States the prime target of terrorism in much the same way as the Europe of czars, kings, and grand dukes was during the period of 1880–1920.[1]

We are living in a dangerous and uncertain time. A breakdown in multilateral cooperation in global politics, accompanying the revival of an overtly violent assertion of U.S. imperial power in the Middle East, has put the fate of millions in the hands of a few as this century begins. At the same time, inequality among nations and within the U.S. continues to grow at a dizzying pace. In response, neoliberal politicians in the U.S. advocate yet more cuts in the budget for social services and public welfare and propose more increases in military and security spending. The twenty-first century is off to a frightening start.

And yet, this dangerous and tragic start also presents opportunities for a renewed politics of equality and democracy within the U.S. and around the world. Neoliberal dominance, seemingly invincible from the fall of the Berlin Wall in 1989 through the 1990s, is under attack as never before. Economic and financial crises—in Mexico in 1994, in Asia in 1997—ignited long-simmering conflicts between wealthy Western creditor nations and the debtor nations of the poorer, developing world. The staggering crash of technology/dot.com stocks listed on the U.S. Nasdaq index punctured the confidence of investors, and gutted the bank accounts of a significant proportion of the American middle class. Resulting public fury helped propel the exposure of corrupt financial practices and widespread corporate greed. And the use of military force in the Middle East exposed the coercive underbelly of purportedly benign U.S. foreign relations and trade policies.

But such disillusionments and exposures will produce opportunities for progressive-left politics only if we are prepared to seize them. This moment of violent rupture in the smooth operations of neoliberal policies might be repaired through the construction of a reformed neoliberal hegemony, rebuilt through brutality and poised to extract yet more of the earth's surplus for the benefit of the wealthiest one percent of the world's population. Or, opposition and resistance to violence and inequality around the world might coalesce into a new social movement strong enough to change our historical course.

There is much encouragement for the hopeful. Highly visible demonstrations against neoliberal globalization beginning in the late 1990s, followed by the rapid assembly of a global peace movement in the early twenty-first century show that visions of a more peaceful, equitable, and democratic world are widely shared. Even some neoliberal "insiders" have begun to see the danger that, to quote the *New York Times*, "capitalists could actually bring down capitalism." Joseph Stiglitz, former chief economist of the World Bank, recently excoriated the "Washington Consensus" for undemocratically and sometimes disastrously imposing "global governance without global government" during the 1980s and 1990s. Republican populist Kevin Phillips listed the costs of the neoliberal "reigning theology" of "free" domestic and global markets to ordinary Americans: reduced income and stagnant wages, long work hours, diminished community and commonweal, fewer private and government services, poor physical and mental health care, competitive consumption, and the spread of money culture values. He also penned the diagnosis of U.S. imperialism as a cause for terrorism that begins this chapter.[2]

Neoliberal insiders wish to save neoliberalism by reforming it, but their alarmist jeremiads provide ample reason for replacing, rather than merely reforming, the institutions and policies that have created the conditions they describe. And so the opportunities for proposing alternate visions, for organizing, and for building something different open up before the progressive-left. But it will not be possible to seize these opportunities without a broad understanding of the neoliberal project—and this understanding will be blocked as long as leftists and campaigners for economic justice dismiss cultural and identity politics as marginal, trivial, or divisive. *Neoliberalism was constructed in and through cultural and identity politics and cannot be undone by a movement without constituencies and analyses that respond directly to that fact. Nor will it be possible to build a new social movement that might be strong, creative, and diverse enough to engage the work of reinventing global politics for the new millennium as long as cultural and identity issues are separated, analytically and organizationally, from the political economy in which they are embedded.*

What the progressive-left must understand is this: Neoliberalism, a late twentieth-century incarnation of Liberalism, organizes material and political life *in terms of* race, gender, and sexuality as well as economic class and nationality, or ethnicity and religion. But the categories through which Liberalism (and thus also neoliberalism) classifies human activity and relationships *actively obscure* the connections among these organizing terms. This abstract claim requires some explanation and illustration and an historical detour. So, in order to pinpoint the specificity of post-1970s neoliberalism, we will first briefly trace the history of Liberalism, then look more closely at the period during which the key terms and categories of Liberalism in the United States were established—the early nineteenth century.

The practices and institutions of exchange known collectively as *capitalism* emerged slowly and unevenly in Anglo-Europe over several centuries as feudal institutions disintegrated. Evolving institutions of production and exchange organized scattered and improvised practices, as centers of innovation shifted across the landscapes of emerging nation-states. The process of change was often dislocating and sometimes violent, and the benefits and costs of the new modes of production and exchange were unequally distributed. By the seventeenth century, the ideas, values, and categories known as *Liberalism* began to cohere into a political theory for capitalist economies administered through nation-states.

Liberal theorists, such as John Locke and Adam Smith, provided a set of metaphors, an organizing narrative, and a moral apologia for capitalism. They also provided a cartography of the "proper" regulation of the relations among the state, the economy, and the population. Liberal theorists disagreed with each other, and their ideas changed over time in relation to changing forms of capitalism and evolving nation-states. But the master terms of Liberalism—*public* vs. *private*—*have* remained relatively consistent, as have the master categories—the *state*, the *economy*, *civil society*, and the *family*. Different forms of Liberalism define the categories somewhat differently and assign publicness and privateness to them in varying ways. But the most public site of collective life under Liberalism is always the state, the "proper" location of publicness, while the most private site is the family. The economy and civil society appear as mixed sites of voluntary, cooperative rational action (as opposed to the coerciveness of the state, and the passion and authority relations of the family), with both public and private functions— though both sites are generally regarded as more private than public. Much of the analytical force of Liberalism then is especially directed toward distinguishing the state from the economy and outlining the proper limits to the state's power to regulate economic, civic, and family life.

The master terms and categories of Liberalism are rhetorical; they do not simply *describe* the "real" world, but rather provide only one way of understanding and organizing collective life. On the one hand, they obscure and mystify many aspects of life under capitalism—hiding stark inequalities of wealth and power and of class, race, gender, and sexuality across nation-states as well as within them. Inequalities are routinely assigned to "private" life, understood as "natural," and bracketed away from consideration in the "public" life of the state. On the other hand, as the ideas of Liberalism become common sense, they also work to *create* or *remake* institutions and practices according to their precepts.[3]

During the early nineteenth century in the United States, Anglo-European Liberalism was adapted to the conditions of the new nation-state. Among the central innovations were the explicit accommodation of the institution of racial slavery and the accompanying assertion of the formal political equality of white men. These innovations proceeded slowly; they were secured in part by *universal white male suffrage*. During the first decades of the nineteenth century, as property qualifications for voting were eliminated in state after state in the U.S., requirements for full citizenship shifted from a complex array of economic, racial, gender, religious, or genealogical characteristics to the simpler identity markers: *whiteness* and *maleness*. This change is often interpreted as an expansion of democracy, because many propertyless white men were newly enfranchised. But the enactment of white male suffrage also constricted democracy. Some propertied women and free black people were newly *dis*enfranchised by the new legislation, but much more significantly, the removal of property considerations from voting requirements allowed for a more complete (rhetorical) separation of the economy, understood as primarily private, from the public, democratically accountable (to white men, in theory) state.[4]

With universal white male suffrage, the formal equality of state participation could more easily be defined as distinct from the "natural,"
"private" inequalities of developing industrial capitalism in the United
States. The identity marker *white* also neatly cordoned off indigenous
populations and non-Anglo-European immigrants from citizenship,
while also working to define the entire institution of racial slavery
as part of the private economy, with slaves counted as property rather
than participants in public life. The identity marker *male* implicitly
cordoned off the family as a private sphere for women and children
under the authority of a white male head of household. Thus enslaved
black people, white women, and their children were defined as belonging (in different ways—slaves as property, white women and children
as subordinates and dependents) to the private worlds governed by individual white men, while indigenous people, nonwhite immigrants,
and free black people occupied ambiguous statuses outside of formal
citizenship.

This particular instantiation of Liberalism in the United States was
never fixed or stable. Its terms and categories never did wholly reflect or
control reality. Liberalism's rhetorical separations of state from economy, civil society, and the family never did describe the real, complex
interrelations of forms of collective life. The workings of the economy depended on the state for support and regulation; civil society
was stratified by economic and political inequalities; the family was
founded on the state-defined and regulated institution of marriage; the
economy provided the material base for state institutions and family
life.[5]

From the early nineteenth century on, the terms "liberal" and "conservative" outlined constantly shifting positions within the overall umbrella of Liberal capitalism in the United States. As slavery gave way to
new forms of racial apartheid and economic inequality, and as the laws
of marriage and the organization of political and economic rights according to gender were challenged and shifted during the late nineteenth and twentieth centuries, notions of the "proper" relations of the

domains of liberalism were debated. "Liberal" and "conservative" positions along the political and cultural spectrums denoted particular, historically specific arguments about those proper relations. For instance, during the Progressive era of the early twentieth century, "liberal" progressives argued to expand the power of the state to regulate economic relations considered at least partly "public," such as the hours and conditions of labor, while "conservatives" considered such regulation an improper interference into "private" property and contract rights.

Radicals of many stripes occasionally attacked the categories themselves, but these challenges were successfully marginalized at each critical phase of the history of American Liberal capitalism. The overarching Liberal distinction between the economy, the state, civil society, and the family consistently shaped, and ultimately disabled progressive-left politics by separating *class politics*—the critique of economic inequality—from *identity politics*—protest against exclusions from national citizenship or civic participation, and against the hierarchies of family life. Though this split is often assigned to post-1968 developments in radical/progressive/left politics, it actually inheres in the categories of Liberalism, in their U.S. version particularly, and has limited the scope of radical politics since the early nineteenth century. Abolitionism and the women's suffrage movement, for instance, only partially overlapped with agrarian radicalism, worker militancy, socialism, or anarchism in the United States.[6]

Competing notions and evaluations of "public" and "private" institutions and "values" organized the political positions we think of as "liberal" and "conservative" as positions *within* Liberalism throughout the nineteenth and twentieth centuries. During the post–World War II period, the contemporary versions of these positions emerged from the battles over the contours of the New Deal and the liberal welfare state and from the Civil Rights movement's challenge to American apartheid.

During the 1950s and 1960s, self-described "conservatives" labeled the New Deal's earlier expansions of public/state action into previously "private" bastions of economic power and civil society or culture as "liberal." The Civil Rights movement's struggle to extend formal public racial equality from the state to "private" employment practices, civil institutions, and public accommodations—for instance, the demand to integrate the customer base as well as employment practices of restaurants, hotels, trains, and buses—was described by opponents as "radical" or "liberal." Though both the New Deal era welfare state and the Civil Rights movement were heterogeneous, with many beliefs and factions contending for effective action, these were commonly lumped together and fiercely attacked by "conservatives" as efforts to expand the state and reduce the freedoms and prerogatives of "private" economic, associational, and family life.

During the 1950s and 1960s, such "conservatives" argued for reprivatizing as much of the common life of the nation as possible. *Except*, in a characteristic contradictory move, conservatives also worked to deny the protections of privacy against state interference in domestic and sexual life to all but the procreative, intraracially married. So, they advocated *more privacy* in the economy and civil society, over and against the interference of the state, but they turned around and advocated *less privacy* in the family and in intimate and sexual life—areas where they supported state interference in the form of laws forbidding or criminalizing miscegenation, abortion and birth control, sodomy, or sexually themed cultural expressions, for instance. Here they were countered by "liberal" efforts to eliminate such laws. Thus, in the arena of economic and collective activities, conservatives represented the state as a bad, coercive, intrusive force against freedom, while New Deal and Keynesian liberals and many leftists invoked a democratically accountable "public" state interest in guaranteeing equality of access, if not always of distribution of material and cultural resources (here liberals and leftists often parted company). In the arena of personal, sexual, and domestic life, conservatives accorded "privacy" only to the favored form of family life and supported state regulation of intimate relations in the name of social order for all others. Liberals ambivalently and unevenly, but increasingly, defended a right to sexual and domestic privacy for all, defined as autonomy or liberty from state interference.

In a larger political, historical, and philosophical frame, the "liberalisms" and "conservatisms" of the 1950s and 1960s were variants of Liberalism—of the kind that has defined the American political project since its inception. But during the 1970s and 1980s, the "liberalism" of the 1950s and 1960s became "old liberalism," "tax and spend liberalism," "welfare state liberalism" or "civil rights and entitlements liberalism." From the dominant political form described by Arthur Schlesinger as "the vital center" in 1949, this liberalism shifted to a left of center position as the new "neoconservatives," former self-identified liberals and leftists themselves, attacked the Civil Rights movement, black radicalism, the growth of the welfare state, the countercultures of the 1960s, the post-1968 new feminism and gay liberation, the New Left, and the Democratic Party, from which many had bolted by 1980. Traditional conservatives, self-identified as such during the 1940s and 1950s, did not easily accept the neocons, who had too recently been tarnished with liberal leanings. But the merging of the neocons into the conservative political and intellectual movement in the United States during the 1980s, along with the election of Ronald Reagan to the presidency, helped to push the perceived "center" in American politics rightward.

During the 1990s a new liberalism appeared, defined against the "old" liberalism, heralded by the New Democrats of the Democratic Leadership Council and led by Bill Clinton. This new liberalism was not a parochial U.S. political formation, but echoed the appearance of "third way" politics in many Western nations—a politics defining itself as somewhere between the "old" liberalism and conservative political parties and policies. Various "third way" parties and leaders labored to combine pro-market, pro-business, "free trade" national and global policies with shrunken remnants of the social democratic and social justice programs of Western welfare states. Third way proponents argued for smaller, more efficient governments operating on business management principles, and appealed to "civil society" (or "the voluntary sector") and "the family" to take up significant roles in the provision of social safety nets.

The new liberal centrism of the 1990s converged with 1980s conservatism in advocating a leaner, meaner government (fewer social services, more "law and order"), a state-supported but "privatized" economy, an invigorated and socially responsible civil society, and a moralized family with gendered marriage at its center. This convergence defined the location "neoliberal"—an expansive center that might include 1990s left/center New Democrats as well as George W. Bush's "compassionate conservatives." Leftists, "old liberals," multiculturalist "special interest" groups, and a right wing composed of religious moralists and overtly racist nationalists (referred to in some quarters as "paleoconservatives") were increasingly marginalized and excluded from political power and mainstream visibility.

Neoliberalism, a political label retrospectively applied to the "conservative" policies of the Reagan and Thatcher regimes in the U.S. and Great Britain, rocketed to prominence as the brand name for the form of pro-corporate, "free market," anti–"big government" rhetoric shaping Western national policy and dominating international financial institutions since the early 1980s. This "neo"liberalism is usually presented not as a particular set of interests and political interventions, but as a kind of nonpolitics—a way of being reasonable, and of promoting universally desirable forms of economic expansion and democratic government around the globe. Who could be against greater wealth and more democracy? Especially since the fall of the Soviet empire by the end of the 1980s, neoliberals have argued that all alternatives to the U.S. model have failed—fascism, communism, socialism, and even the relatively mild forms of the welfare state advocated by social democrats, labor movements, and Keynesians. Not trumpeted are the sharply declining participation rates in the Western "democracies," and the rapidly expanding, vast economic inequalities that neoliberal policies have generated in the U.S., in Great Britain, and globally.

In world politics, Western political leaders and economic elites have supported neoliberal policies as the apogee of private freedoms and maximum wealth expansion within a neutral regulatory framework. But in practice, the institutions promulgating neoliberal solutions to global problems have advanced the specific interests of Western financial, commercial, and trade centers with coercive tools—especially through offering conditioned loans to needy nations, and by negotiating and imposing biased trade agreements. The practices of the International Monetary Fund, the World Bank, and the World Trade Organization have resulted not in a "neutral" global framework for economic and cultural flows, as the term "globalization" implies, but rather in the transfer of wealth and power from poor parts of the world to the West, especially to the United States during the 1990s. As even neoliberal "insider" critics have pointed out, global financial institutions have acted primarily in the direct interests of Western creditors and corporations, transferring wealth from the globe's poorest to its richest locations. These practices constitute a reinvention of Western imperialism, not the worldwide democratization and broad-based enrichment promised by neoliberal globalization's promoters.[7]

This neoliberalism is generally associated with economic and trade policy; the cultural politics of neoliberalism are considered and debated relatively rarely, primarily in discussions of the economic and political mechanisms of U.S. and Western cultural imperialism. In the domestic arena, the "culture wars" of the past twenty years have been conducted separately from questions of monetary and fiscal policy, trade negotiations and economic indicators—the recognized realm of neoliberal policy. But in a wide range of cultural policy territories—from public spending for culture and education, to the "moral" foundations for welfare reform, from affirmative action to marriage and domestic partnership debates—neoliberalism's profoundly antidemocratic and anti-egalitarian agenda has shaped public discussion. Neoliberalism in fact *has* a cultural politics—a contradictory and contested cultural politics, not unlike the equally contradictory and internally contested economic and trade politics that have defined the location "neoliberal" since the Reagan/Thatcher 1980s.[8]

The broadest cultural project of neoliberalism—the transforming of global cultures into "market cultures"—has a mixed track record. Both in the U.S. and worldwide, neoliberal efforts to establish or re-make the relations among the core domains of Western liberalism—the state, the economy, the family and civil society—rarely succeed in a straightforward way. While posing as the harbingers of peace and pros-perity for the global masses, neoliberal policymakers in fact create peace in some places and war in others, prosperity for some and ecological destruction and poverty for many more. Target populations and insti-tutions do not cooperate; people welcome, adapt to, or resist the impo-sitions of neoliberal change in unpredictable ways. But overall, efforts to create a world safe for neoliberalism have been most successful where the domains of Western liberalism have been successfully imposed or redescribed through neoliberalism's key terms: *privatization* and *per-sonal responsibility*. These terms define the central intersections be-tween the *culture* of neoliberalism and its economic vision, in the U.S. and abroad (see the case studies in chapters 2 and 3).

The primary strategy of turn-of-the-millennium neoliberalism is *privatization*, the term that describes the transfer of wealth and deci-sion-making from public, more-or-less accountable decision-making bodies to individual or corporate, unaccountable hands. Neoliberals advocate privatization of economic enterprises, which they consider fundamentally "private" and inappropriately placed in any "public" arena. They go further than this, though, in advocating that many os-tensibly public services and functions also be placed in private profit-making hands—education, garbage collection, prison building and operation, and cultural production. All this privacy is rendered desir-able by the recycling and updating of nineteenth-century liberalism's equation of economic activity with voluntary, uncoerced, private free-dom, and with productivity, efficiency, and wealth expansion.

This private world appears as an imaginary construction, not a his-torical reality. Inefficient, unprofitable "private" industries routinely request and receive government support, even direct subsidies. And the greater "productivity" of some privatized services depends on the substitution of lower-paid workers and lower-quality materials rather than on any managerial acumen. Thus the allegedly free and efficient private-enterprise system operates, not as an empirical reality, but rather as a phantom ideal that is then contrasted with coercive, plod-ding, incompetent, intrusive post–World War II governments—from fallen totalitarian regimes to stagnant or bankrupt welfare states.

Of course, this rhetorical universe in no way matches the "really ex-isting" policies of neoliberal politicians, who often advocate govern-ment support for "private" industries, regulated economic competition to soften the effects of "free" market discipline, and a range of welfare state programs (especially those that benefit more affluent, voting pop-ulations). In actual policy debates, the project of applying the operative rhetorics of public and private can thus become quite complex. When the state acts to support "private" business interests—providing subsi-dies and bailouts for instance—that can be good. But when the state acts in the "public" interest—providing housing for the poor or pro-tection for the environment—that can be intrusive, coercive, and bad. The proper range for debate over government action is understood as relatively narrow, covering monetary, fiscal and trade policies, infras-tructure maintenance, and "night watchman" property protection, law and order measures. Thus, in comparison with the mid–twentieth cen-tury Western welfare states, that expanded state action to provide a "so-cial safety net" and new support for public institutions, neoliberalism shrinks the scope of equality and democratic public life dramatically, in all areas of material production and distribution.

In the policy arenas of cultural and personal life, neoliberalism is currently more pointedly conflicted. Ranging from New Democrats to "compassionate conservatives," neoliberal politicians and organizations debate the relative merits of a more-or-less liberal, libertarian, or socially conservative agenda. Most flexibly combine apparently contradictory positions, in a kind of productive incoherence designed to appeal and appease: President Bill Clinton, for example, supported affirmative action and the death penalty, abortion rights, and the Defense of Marriage Act. But the debate and continuing flexibility in these arenas, particularly in the U.S., is working toward a "third way" rhetoric positioned between the moral conservatism of the religious and nationalist right, and the perceived "multiculturalism" and "civil rights agenda" of the progressive-left. This rhetoric promotes the *privatization* of the costs of social reproduction, along with the care of human dependency needs, through *personal responsibility* exercised in the family and in civil society—thus shifting costs from state agencies to individuals and households. This process accompanies the call for tax cuts that deplete public coffers, but leave more money in the "private" hands of the wealthy.

The valorized concepts of *privatization* and *personal responsibility* travel widely across the rhetorics of contemporary policy debates, joining economic goals with cultural values while obscuring the identity politics and upwardly redistributive impetus of neoliberalism. Two general policy arenas have proved especially productive for these concepts and help to illustrate the relationship between the economic policies and the cultural projects of neoliberalism—welfare "reform" and "law and order" initiatives. In both arenas, neoliberals have promoted "private" *competition, self-esteem,* and *independence* as the roots of *personal responsibility,* and excoriated "public" *entitlement, dependency,* and *irresponsibility* as the sources of social ills. And in both arenas, state policies reflect and enact identity and cultural politics invested in hierarchies of race, gender, and sexuality as well as class and nationality.

Welfare reform and the law and order politics of the past two decades clearly illustrate the dense interrelations among neoliberalism's economic vision and its cultural projects. *The goal of raising corporate profits has never been pursued separately from the rearticulation of hierarchies of race, gender, and sexuality in the United States and around the globe.* Neoliberals, unlike many leftists and progressives, simply don't assume that there is any important difference between material goals and identity politics. They make use of identity politics to obscure redistributive aims, and they use "neutral" economic policy terms to hide their investments in identity-based hierarchies, but they don't make the mistake of fundamentally accepting the ruse of liberalism—the assertion of a clear boundary between the politics of identity and class.[9]

During the 1990s, welfare "reform" made it onto the legislative agenda as the long-term culmination of one of many efforts to cut social costs, in the form of state-funded entitlements, and cut labor costs—thereby boosting the corporate profits that had begun sliding in the 1960s and 1970s, slowly rose again in the 1980s, then skyrocketed in the 1990s. Few put this underlying agenda of the "workfare" component of welfare "reform" as bluntly as political science professor Lawrence Meade when he wrote,

> Low-wage work apparently must be mandated, just as a draft has sometimes been necessary to staff the military. Authority achieves compliance more efficiently than benefits, at least from society's viewpoint. Government need not make the desired behavior worthwhile to people.[10]

Part of a broader cultural project of legitimating the redistribution of resources upward, welfare "reform" has also depended, for its cultural effectiveness, on coded hierarchies of race, gender, and sexuality—especially as they affect women and children.

The overall impetus of welfare "reform," or the elimination of the so-called welfare "entitlement," was to transfer the function of providing a social safety net from public agencies to private households maintained through low-wage employment. The gap between the needs of workers and their dependents, and the inadequate pay and benefits provided by their insecure, often no-benefits jobs, is left to be filled by overstretched families and overburdened volunteer charities. Thus social service functions are *privatized* through *personal responsibility* as the proper functions of the state are narrowed, tax and wage costs in the economy are cut, and more social costs are absorbed by civil society and the family. In addition, this redistribution of costs and benefits has been starkly differentiated by hierarchies of race, gender, and sexuality.

In some respects neoliberal welfare reform, crystallized in the 1996 Personal Responsibility and Work Opportunity Reconciliation Act (PRWORA), was nothing new. From early-twentieth-century widows' pensions to the 1935 Social Security Act and Aid to Dependent Children (ADC), which morphed into Aid to Families with Dependent Children (AFDC), welfare policy in the United States has always been shaped to reflect racial exclusions and racist assumptions, to police the "morality" of poor women, and to regulate and contain the low-wage labor market. The 1996 revamping of AFDC into Temporary Assistance for Needy Families (TANF), one of the centerpiece achievements of the New Democrats under President Bill Clinton, did not break this pattern. The Democratic effort to "end welfare as we know it" *did* mask the race- and gender-specific operations of the policy change with neutral goals like promoting "self-esteem" and "empowerment" through work "opportunity." But as political analyst Anna Marie Smith has clearly demonstrated, the actual policies of the legislation (including "family caps" to limit support for newborns, mandatory child support cooperation even in cases of domestic violence, family planning and adoption relinquishment incentives, and sexual abstinence education) expose its underlying assumption: The sexual practices and household structures of poor women, especially black women, are the central causes of poverty and of associated social disorder and criminality.[11]

These legislative features emerged from decades of efforts to erode New Deal welfare state programs, especially AFDC, through the deployment of images of sexually promiscuous, lazy welfare queens breeding for the profit of an ever-enlarging welfare check. The specific neoliberal spin on this cultural project was the removal of explicitly racist, misogynist language and images, and the substitution of the language and values of *privatization* and *personal responsibility*. From the Clinton administration into the Bush II regime, welfare reform has been presented as a boon to recipients lifted out of welfare *dependency* and into the low-wage labor market. The new policies have also been touted as helping to promote marriage and reduce youthful "out of wedlock" pregnancy.

Welfare reform advocates do not trumpet the transfer of costs for care of children (and for the ill and the elderly, who are also often cared for by unpaid or low-paid women at home) from the public purse to the lowest paid women workers as the goal of new legislation. "Compassionate conservatives" do not connect the goal of tax cutting for businesses and the estates of the wealthiest Americans to such cost reductions. And though the value of sexual abstinence followed by marriage is accepted across the entire expanse of the neoliberal political spectrum, from traditional moralists to earnest communitarian progressives, the cornerstone role of marriage as a coercive tool of the privatization of social costs is not exactly clearly outlined.

In neoliberal discourse, married women are assumed to be responsible for children and dependent on wage-earning husbands, and are often advised to stay at home during their children's early years to build self-esteem and independence in the young. They are also encouraged to volunteer, as the bulwarks of civil society and "faith-based" social service provisions, with their unpaid labor underpinning the *privatized* social safety net. Single, divorced, and widowed women may "choose" to work in a gender and race-segmented labor market without affordable childcare or public assistance in order to build *their* self-esteem and independence—or, some welfare reformers suggest, they may "choose" to put their children up for adoption by married couples, or house them in orphanages. Lesbian and gay, bisexual or transgendered parents may choose only to take their chances amid the patchwork legal minefield of inadequate to hostile partnership provisions, custody rulings, adoptions laws, social services, employment and health insurance practices, and educational (in)visibility.

For men, neoliberal policy wonks and politicians have advocated "law and order" programs, including the "war on crime" and the "war on drugs," "zero tolerance" policing, "quality of life" crackdowns on crimes against public order, and the mass incarceration of young poor men, especially black men.

As Christian Parenti, Angela Davis, and other critics of the U.S. "prison industrial complex" have pointed out, the rise in mass imprisonment in the U.S., leading to the highest incarceration rates in the world, proceeded in two waves: The first, under President Richard Nixon, began as a response to widespread political rebellion and the perceived precariousness of social, racial, and economic order; the second, under President Ronald Reagan, was designed as a response to the poverty and dislocation created through neoliberal economic restructuring. Setting aside the use of social democratic government programs as a primary mode of incorporating and defusing the anger and alienation of poor populations, neoliberal policymakers turned instead to policing and imprisonment as central regulatory and disciplinary institutions. Social democracy's social safety net, negotiated through protracted struggles among social classes and racial groups from the 1930s to the 1960s, had redistributed a proportion of accumulating wealth and power down and outward. Once corporate profits began to slip during the 1960s, political rhetoric and favored modes of social control got harder and meaner.[12]

Law and order policies have been promoted with race and gender "neutral" rhetoric emphasizing the threat of crime to "average" citizens, even as actual crime rates have declined. But the impact of such policies has been far from neutral, as a close look at the coded language of politics clearly reveals. As H. R. Haldeman once commented,

> [President Nixon] emphasized that you have to face the fact that the whole problem is really the blacks. The key is to devise a system that recognizes this while not appearing to.[13]

By the year 2000, fully half of U.S. prisoners were black (while African-Americans constituted 13 percent of the U.S. population), and nearly one-quarter of young black men were incarcerated or subject to the criminal justice system through parole and probation. Those convicted of felonies were permanently barred from voting in twelve states. Immigrant populations, or citizens perceived as immigrant or "foreign," were subjected to increased surveillance and harassment by the Immigration and Naturalization Service, as well as by border patrols and federal, state, and local law enforcement agencies, following the anti-immigrant sentiment codified in the passage of Proposition 187 in California. This harassment then escalated after September 11, 2001. The vast majority of those affected by such aggressive policing and incarceration practices have been men of color—perceived as less docile because less encumbered by responsibility for children, more violent, and therefore less productive for the "private" low-wage workforce than women.

The current crisis of neoliberalism in the United States, marked by spreading corruption scandals, slipping corporate profits and declining foreign direct investment, is throwing the conflicts among mainstream economic and political elites into sharp relief. On one side are the "free market" true believers, the descendants of F. A. Hayek and Milton Friedman who once formed a small unpopular minority, but grew into a kind of secular priesthood by the 1990s. This variety of utopianism is represented in its purist form by the Cato Institute's vision of a libertarian market society, in which the state, the family, and civil society are best shaped by market values. By the mid-1990s, both rationalistic New Democratic policy wonks and demagogic Republicans lying deep in the swamp of hysterical populist moralism seemed drawn toward the light of such market utopianism. Just following the Newt Gingrich–led Republican sweep of the House of Representatives in 1994, noted swamp monster and new majority leader in the House, Representative Dick Armey, spoke at the dedication of the new Hayek auditorium at the CATO Institute, saying,

> Fifty years after *The Road to Serfdom*, the closing thought of F. A. Hayek's great treatise (as expressed in the highly influential *Reader's*

Digest condensation) still rings true: "The guiding principle of any attempt to create a world of free men is this: A policy of freedom for the individual is the only truly progressive policy...."

I mean, who would have imagined, a year ago, that the leaders of Congress would be looking to those crazy libertarians over at Cato for advice? Who could have imagined we would be discussing abolishing whole programs, turning others back to the states, repealing ill-conceived laws, and dismantling cabinet agencies, just as you've always recommended?[14]

Who indeed would have thought that Hayek and the *Reader's Digest* would have been brought into communion? Or that a moral regulator of Armey's ferocity would be so well received among libertarian opponents of U.S. drug laws? Or that "ending welfare as we know it" would soon become the signal achievement of a "progressive" Democratic administration? Such were the strange convergences of the 1990s.

But the current crisis of neoliberalism is now bringing other conflicts, buried under market frenzy during the 1990s, into the political light. Hard-line Republican neoliberals in the U.S. government have begun to advocate violence and war abroad, as well as increasing disciplinary surveillance at home, as modes of ensuring the stability of Western corporate and political hegemony. On the other side, softer neoliberals have come out swinging in the name of "democracy" and global cooperative multilateralism. Neo-Keynesians, progressives, populists, and social democrats support reformed international institutions and diplomacy in U.S. foreign and trade relations. They also support renewed forms of welfare state power to rein in market abuses and the sometimes violent as well as unjust anarchy that insufficiently regulated markets spawn. Even neoliberal true believers, from the editors of *The Economist* to Wall Street denizens, have shifted gears to support more state action to rescue capitalism from a feared global free fall. The political question within the neoliberal fold is: Will state action take the form of global warfare, corporate welfare, or a renewed, limited social democracy?[15]

The newly more visible conflict among elites is accompanied by an overlapping conflict over cultural politics. On one side is the residual strategy of cultural traditionalism deployed during the late twentieth century "culture wars"—energetic attacks against "multiculturalism" and "permissiveness" intended to shrink the funding bases as well as popular support for sites of nonmarket politics—the arts, education, and social services. On the other side is a newly emergent "equality" politics that supports "diversity" and "tolerance," but defines these in the narrowest terms, and entirely within the framework of globalist neoliberalism.

2

The Incredible
Shrinking Public

During November 1997, the Women's Studies Program at the State University of New York (SUNY) at New Paltz sponsored a relatively ordinary annual conference—Revolting Behavior: The Challenges of Women's Sexual Freedom. Such conferences, emphasizing issues of women's sexuality, diversity, and dissent, had once been hotly controversial. During 1982, the ninth annual Barnard College conference in the series called The Scholar and the Feminist had unintentionally focused such controversy into a widely publicized, notorious encounter among feminists with widely divergent views on a range of sexual issues—sadomasochism, butch/femme lesbian cultures, and state regulation of pornography and prostitution among them.[1] This high tide of controversy settled into calmer ripples of debate during the next decade, and by 1997 conferences dealing with such issues were no longer hot spots, but had become more routine airings and rehearsals of continuing feminist exploration and conflict over sexual practices and politics.

The "sex wars" debates that raged during this period, roughly from the late 1970s through the early 1990s, primarily engaged feminists, both activists and academics, and consumed the attention of the feminist and alternative press. More mainstream constituencies and media jumped in only for a shorter stretch of time, primarily during the legislative battles over a feminist authored antipornography ordinance during the mid- 1980s—though there has been some heat generated periodically over the issue of prostitution as well.[2] Mainstream interest in sexual controversies and the distorted and displacing energies of sexualized hysteria shifted to AIDS and arts censorship debates and to child sexuality and sexual abuse issues during the mid- to late-1980s and into the 1990s. Gay men, "satanistic" day care providers, sexually violent predators, and erotic art replaced the feminist sex wars as primary sites of panic and publicity.[3]

But in 1997, a women's studies conference on sexuality, similar to scores of others convened over the previous decade, ignited a political firestorm in the state of New York. Though located well out of range of any media capital, at a bucolic upstate SUNY campus and not an elite New York City college, the media blitz surrounding the conference and the controversy nonetheless fed the escalating feeding frenzy of widening layers of local to national press, from the *New York Times* to the *Chronicle of Higher Education*, including National Public Radio and finally television coverage—by spring 1998, Mike Wallace could be found improbably reading a lesbian safer-sex pamphlet that had been distributed at the conference to SUNY New Paltz's president Roger Bowen before the national audience of CBS's *60 Minutes* news magazine show.[4]

This attention was completely unexpected. The women's studies program had been accustomed to objections to their programming lodged by the critics of "political correctness" and "multiculturalism" on college campuses, active in New York as well as nationally since 1990. And they expected the overwrought and fantastic attacks of local gadfly Peter Shipley and his right-wing "group," Truth in Politics—Shipley had been dogging their events regularly and was just as regularly ignored. Such criticisms and attacks were routine by 1997, and sometimes damaging,[5] but a full-scale sex panic seemed nowhere on the horizon when Revolting Behavior was planned.

Here is how it began: SUNY trustee Candace de Russy and her husband, Cortes, attended the conference "at the behest of concerned New Paltz citizens," possibly including Shipley, who also showed up, along with SUNY New Paltz College Council member George Morton. She was joined by right-wing pundit and *New Criterion* managing editor Roger Kimball. The following day, de Russy dashed off a memo to her fellow trustees and to SUNY chancellor John Ryan detailing her observations at the "disturbing" workshops and presentations she witnessed. The one-day conference included a plenary session, a performance event, a reception, and more than twenty workshops, including HIV Education: A Community Affair; Reproductive Rights and Women's Freedom; Marriage and Sexuality: Traditional and Changing Patterns in Africa; Sexuality and the Literature of Black Women; The Effect of Religion on Women's Sexual Experience; A Soltar la Cruz: Reclaiming Our Bodies and Our Sexuality; and Sexual Choices in the 1990s: Young Women Speak Out. But de Russy mostly avoided the lecture- or presentation-style workshops and showed a marked preference for the hands-on demonstration workshops. There were only a few. De Russy's choices included Safe, Sane and Consensual S/M; Sex Toys for Women; Queer Sexuality: A Spectrum of Women's Choices; and the performance by Shelly Mars, "Whiplash: Tales of a Tomboy."

As a conservative Republican and a devout Catholic, de Russy was *outraged*. In addition to writing her memo to the trustees and chancellor Ryan, she contacted her many associates and whipped them into action—most notably New York governor Pataki, who had appointed her to the SUNY board of trustees, and conservative Republican state legislators John Guerin and Thomas Kirwin. Meanwhile, by the following Wednesday, November 5, Kimball had penned a screed for the *Wall Street Journal* excitedly describing his conference experience. Headlined "A Syllabus for Sickos," Kimball's column described the same workshops and performance event as de Russy's memo, then went on to opine that,

> Among the many issues that events like "Revolting Behavior" raise, two stand out. One is a deep moral issue that concerns the appropriate place of sexuality in human life. Behind the celebration of "Sex Toys for Women" and other such phenomena is a vision of sexuality totally emancipated from nature. It is a fundamentally narcissistic vision, informed by the radical ethos of the 1960s, that looks

to sex as an instrument of political emancipation and personal beautitude. Again and again at the conference, speakers asserted that sexual identity was essentially a "social construction," infinitely malleable and morally neutral. "Shame" was everywhere presented as the enemy of liberation.

But as elsewhere in life, the single-minded pursuit of sexual pleasure turns out to be profoundly dehumanizing. The person without shame is not liberated but merely shameless. There was a lot of talk about "sexual autonomy" at New Paltz last weekend. But the conference made clear that when human sexuality truly becomes "autonomous," it descends into the chilly province of sex toys and sadomasochism.

In this way Kimball rehearsed a run-of-the-mill "culture wars" attack on 1960s sexual "license," and on post-1970s theories critiquing the naturalness and historical permanence of fixed sexual identities. Or as Kimball put these familiar objections, "'Revolting Behavior' was in fact a celebration of perversity and sexual libertinage." And that, his readers were to understand, was a very bad thing.

De Russy and Kimball hyped the sexual images to inflame politicians, taxpayers, and parents to stop this waste of state funds at a public university. But right away, the firestorm they ignited acquired a peculiar focus—de Russy and Kimball, then state legislators Guerin and Kirwin, along with college council member Morton, and of course joined by the obsessive, peculiar, and previously ineffective Shipley, organized a campaign to have Roger Bowen removed as president of the SUNY New Paltz campus. Press releases and phone campaigns, political networking and media spinning all revved up to fire Bowen. The details of the November 1 conference, along with inflammatory descriptions of a conference sponsored by the School of Fine and Performing Arts at SUNY New Paltz on November 7–8, Subject to Desire: Refiguring the Body, were adduced as evidence of Bowen's irresponsibility and unfitness for his post.[6]

Never mind that Bowen had not been involved in organizing either conference, and that the Office of the President had contributed only a small fraction of the funds for Revolting Behavior (about $400 of a nearly $6,000 budget), or that he publicly stated that he found some of the conference events "offensive" or "in poor taste."[7] The spreading media frenzy and political uproar centered on the question of Bowen's responsibility for permitting the women's studies program to present a conference that, in the words of the conservative culture warriors' National Association of Scholars executive director Bradford Wilson, "abandoned all scholarly pretense by bringing in sex trade entrepreneurs and propagandists to offer training in the huff-and-puff of lesbian sadomasochism and the use of sex toys."[8]

Some of the attacks on Bowen were strangely personal, as when Tom Carroll, president of an antitax business lobbying organization called Change, New York, was quoted in the *New York Times* saying, "Bowen then can do whatever he wants, with whomever he wants, no matter how deviant, with his own money." The confused implication being, apparently, that Bowen was something like a lesbian sadomasochist? But most centered on his alleged failure to fulfill the role of a chief executive officer, and exercise control over the behavior of "his" faculty, the content of campus programming, and the use of (even very small amounts) of public money.

The orchestrated uproar over the conference, and the calls for Bowen's resignation, led Governor Pataki to call the conference "outrageous" and to ask Chancellor Ryan for a report on its propriety and legality as well as for recommendations on how to prevent similar events from occurring at New York's public universities. Ryan appointed a panel of four current and former high-level SUNY officials and a faculty representative to undertake the investigation and make the recommendations. But when a draft of the panel's report was leaked to the *New York Times*, the campaign against Bowen ran into its first major obstacle—the report exonerated Bowen, indirectly slammed the conference attackers, and defended sponsorship of the conference on the grounds of academic freedom, arguing that,

To permit the presence of public tax support to impose limitations on academic freedom would imperil at almost all postsecondary institutions the freedom to follow ideas to their conclusion and invite into the institution a wide range of perspectives for consideration and debate.[9]

The defense of Bowen and SUNY New Paltz on the grounds of academic freedom was the most popular tactical move among organizations and supporters in the mainstream press and was the argument favored by Bowen himself. Invoking academic freedom allowed defenders of the conference to ignore its content or to criticize it as did Bowen, arguing that toleration of "offensive" views was a price worth paying for maintaining the university's role as an open forum in a democracy. The SUNY New Paltz Faculty Senate and the United University Professors, the union representing faculty and professionals throughout the SUNY system, voted support for Bowen and the principle of academic freedom. Support also rolled in from anticensorship and free speech organizations, including the New York branch of the ACLU and the National Coalition Against Censorship. The American Association of University Professors conferred its academic freedom award on President Bowen. And "in support of free speech," an anonymous couple donated $350,000 to help complete SUNY New Paltz's Samuel Dorsky Museum of Art, as a form of moral support for Bowen in the wake of the conference fracas.[10]

The defense of Revolting Behavior on the grounds of academic freedom was on one level crucial to the protection and survival of the Women's Studies Program at SUNY New Paltz, but on another level such defenses were small comfort. If Bowen was shored up as the guardian of free inquiry on campus, the conference organizers were left holding the bag of alleged irresponsibility, poor judgment, low standards, or even prurience and sponsorship of "perversion" among students.

Defenders of the conference itself, its goals and content, were many fewer than the upholders of academic freedom—but there were some.

The women's studies program valiantly defended itself, issuing press releases and organizing follow-up events to discuss the controversy and try to understand its roots and impact. Conference organizer and women's studies professor Amy Kesselman pointed out the distortions in the attackers' descriptions of the conference and argued that the conference was controversial because "women as sexual objects are commonplace, women as sexual subjects or actors are controversial, or threatening." In an "Open Letter Concerning the Assault on the Women's Conference," Herman and Julia Schwendinger, professors of sociology and criminology at SUNY New Paltz, respectively, argued that the attacks were part of a backlash against the feminist movement. And the National Coalition for Sexual Freedom congratulated the women's studies program for "taking an active part in the development of feminist politics on sexuality and demystifying alternative practices." In addition, several organizations and publications of students, faculty, or other supporters in the CUNY as well as the SUNY system discussed and declared support for the conference—for the significance of the content, as well as for the principle of academic freedom.[11]

None of these defenses stopped the attack, which continued into the spring of 1998. In a January 12, 1998, radio address trustee de Russy compared the New Paltz conference to rallies of "neo-Nazi skinheads" and "a celebration of female circumcision and ritual animal slaughter" and concluded that,

> President Bowen and its other defenders have emptied academic freedom of all its dignity. They have suspended judgment, standards, scientific inquiry, and critical thinking. They have also abandoned common sense and decency.

De Russy was later joined in this kind of attack by more nationally known radio personalities, including Rush Limbaugh and Dr. Laura. Meanwhile, Chancellor Ryan ignored his own appointed panel's report, failing to even mention it when he accused Bowen of "errors of judgment" that "caused harm and embarrassment to the New Paltz campus and the State University" at a January 1998 SUNY Board of Trustees meeting. Ryan summarized his view, saying,

> While the complexities of sexuality from many perspectives are clearly appropriate matters for academic study and discourse, the New Paltz conference promulgated a "how to do it" manual on lesbianism and sadomasochism—not at all appropriate for a university.

Following Ryan's remarks, the SUNY Board of Trustees voted to "neither accept or reject" the "Review into Women's Studies Conference at SUNY/New Paltz, November 1, 1997" that had exonerated Bowen.[12]

In February, individuals and organizations associated with the attack on the conference began making numerous requests for SUNY New Paltz public documents under the Freedom of Information Act. Change, New York—an organization counting De Russy among its publicly prominent members—requested course syllabi and the credentials of Women's Studies Program and School of Fine and Performing Arts professors, along with budget, contract, and hiring and promotions documents. This fishing expedition inspired considerable anxiety on the New Paltz campus. As Vince Aceto, president of SUNY's Faculty Senate, commented, "They are just harassing the campus to hell."[13]

But what was the ultimate agenda for such harassment? Most mainstream reporting framed the whole scenario as another battle in the decade long "culture wars" on college campuses. This was clearly the framing for the March 60 Minutes segment that opened with Candace de Russy calling the SUNY New Paltz conference "a travesty of academic standards." The overall segment placed the conference controversy within the context of debate over the place and value of lesbian and gay studies, queer theory, and sexuality education at colleges and

universities. According to Wallace and company, the issue was sex—
what's normal? And what's appropriate for college classrooms and
sponsored events on campus? Thus the assumed central relevance of
Bowen's reaction to Wallace's on-camera reading of passages from *The
Safer Sex Handbook for Lesbians.*

This framing for the controversy did capture one of its central log-
ics: Hysteria and panic over nonnormative sexuality played a central
role in whipping up opposition to progressive curricula and to decentralized faculty and student initiative in planning courses and events,
which in turn were two important targets of the 1990s campus culture
wars. The "sides" of the debate as they were framed on *60 Minutes* pit-
ted support for increased control over campus intellectual life in the
name of "academic responsibility" on one side, versus support for innovation, exploration, and responsiveness to student as well as faculty
interest in the name of "academic freedom" on the other. The role of
minority, dissident, and highly stigmatized sexualities in these "culture
wars" battles was to inflame the public on behalf of the right, and constrain or disable the left's response. Because no one was able, willing, or
permitted to directly defend lesbian s/m in mainstream venues in 1997,
progressive champions of cultural diversity were limited to arguing for
the staid and seemingly tepid values of academic freedom, or for free
speech, as alarmist advocates of "responsibility" paraded unfamiliar
and highly charged images before an alternately stunned, frightened,
and fascinated public. In this way "charges" involving the "promotion"
of such practices worked similarly to charges of communist subversion
during the high tide of cold war hysteria.

But this widespread framing of the debate as a "culture wars" con-
frontation missed both the revealing local details of the conference controversy and the larger political and economic context in which this
battle, as well as other "culture wars" debates, was embedded. Why, for
instance, were attacks on the conference immediately mobilized into
calls for Roger Bowen's resignation as president of the SUNY New
Paltz campus? This question was not raised in national or even state
and local mainstream reporting. But Alisa Solomon, a CUNY faculty

member writing for the *Village Voice*, immediately made the connections from De Russy to Change, New York, to years of attacks on public higher education in New York. Solomon placed the fiasco in the context of the rise of Republican fiscal conservatism in New York State since the election of George Pataki in 1995 and to concerted efforts since then to downsize or eliminate public institutions, in the name of cutting business taxes and creating a more pro-business climate in the state. Headlined "Sexual Smokescreen," Solomon began, "When there's scant support for your campaign to downsize public institutions, seek out the sex—especially when it's female or gay."[14]

The keys to understanding the attack on the conference are the links that Solomon illuminated in her November, 1997 article between culture, politics, and economics—links that come to light in specific local efforts, such as the attack on the conference, that connect with many other such efforts to form a uniquely articulated set of arguments and strategies. The relevant links from the conference controversy to New York politics to neoliberalism's overall goals take the focus from sex in education through Republican Party politics to the shifting priorities and alignments of U.S.-based businesses during the 1990s.

In New York in the late 1990s, a neoliberal policy agenda had only recently clearly replaced the agenda of "old tax and spend liberalism," represented by the previous governor of New York, Mario Cuomo. Though Cuomo had, like Bill Clinton, forwarded the neoliberal business agenda during his years as governor, unlike Clinton, he had also periodically and crucially resisted it.[15] With the election of conservative Republican George Pataki, such resistance had been largely swept from many state level institutions as downsizing and privatization, along with tax cutting and "welfare" shrinkage became policy priorities. To forward the neoliberal vision of a shrunken and pacified public university, Pataki packed the SUNY Board of Trustees with activists, including Candace de Russy.

But attacking popular programs and institutions required a public relations campaign as well as government initiative—and public education remained widely popular in New York State. To assist in the public media strategy in support of neoliberalism in state politics, Change, New York—an association of CEOs of major business enterprises, investment bankers, and stockbrokers with Republican Party connections that had significantly supported the Pataki campaign— established the Empire Foundation for Policy Research. The foundation released three reports during summer 1997 attacking SUNY for being "too costly and elaborate." [16]

Both Change, New York and the Empire Foundation had culture warriors on their boards—with a chain of networked associations including the National Association of Scholars, the American Council of Alumni and Trustees, the Manhattan Institute, the Olin Foundation, and the Madison Institute for Educational Affairs. These organizations and individuals connected with them orchestrated a long campaign against CUNY as well as SUNY during the 1990s. According to a later article by Solomon also in the *Village Voice*,

> Though it plays out differently at the upstate and city schools, the strategy of those who would shrink both systems repeats the tactic that succeeded so well in the drive to eliminate welfare: The best way to reduce expenditures of tax-levied funds, the logic goes, is to demonize the beneficiaries of that spending.[17]

Attacks against CUNY thus tended to adopt the racially coded strategies of the antiwelfare campaign, portraying the predominantly minority, immigrant, and poor student populations served there as lazy and undeserving. Against SUNY, where the majority of students are white and working or middle class (though nearly one-third are members of racial minorities), attackers adopted a strategy from the assaults on the National Endowment for the Arts and looked for sex.

Thus the "culture wars" tactic of attacking the vulnerable outer edges of progressive institutions, at points where public support is weakest, was joined to the overall goals of a conservative think tank like the Empire Foundation, self-described as an "independent research foundation" established to "develop policies to stimulate economic growth and jobs in New York state and to get the state's fiscal house in order." The ambitious de Russy had laid out a plan for precisely this merged agenda in a 1995 memo to the SUNY trustees. Entitled "A Personal Vision of SUNY's Future," the memo included the headings "Refocus What Is Taught at SUNY and How," "Reduce Taxpayer Subsidies," "More Active Role in Selecting Campus Presidents," and "Review Race- and Sex-Based Preferences." Specific listed goals included rank ordering the campuses in preparation for closings and mergers, requiring greater faculty productivity as part of union negotiations, raising tuition, reversing policies limiting privatization and identifying opportunities to reduce the tax burden, eliminating English-as-a-second-language courses, and reviewing affirmative action policies in light of California's 1995 rejection of the state university's race- and sex-based programs. And—crucially shaping the coming campaign for Roger Bowen's resignation—reasserting the Board's "proper" role in selecting campus presidents.[18]

De Russy voted against Bowen's appointment as president of the SUNY New Paltz campus in 1996 on procedural grounds, but later admitted a "philosophical difference" with him. Previously a professor of international affairs specializing in Japan, as well as an administrator at Hollins College, Bowen considered himself aligned with the classic values of academic culture, understood as uneasily at odds with political and economic values, and precariously if necessarily separated from them. He was regarded as something of a holdout in the zealous campaign to corporatize SUNY, and his removal became a focus for SUNY trustees and others sharing the Change, New York vision for public higher education. The attacks on Bowen did not drive him away immediately (he did not resign until 2001); they served to mobilize support for him and to motivate him to make his critique of the forces undermining SUNY explicit. In a May 2001 address to the United University Professors assembly of delegates in Albany, just before his departure more than four years after the conflagration over his stewardship of SUNY New Paltz, Bowen delivered his most pointed and aggressive summary of this critique:

Conflict has originated, I believe, from the corporatization of higher education, which in turn is a result of the boom economy of the 1990s and the simultaneous collapse of Soviet bloc socialism. The triumph of capitalism and socialism's crippling reinforced the superiority of the market as the informing principle of politics. The market's hidden hand tolerates no wasted motion. Its deftness in allocation of scarce resources—this is what I mean by politics— invariably results in a form of distributive justice that no longer brooks serious debate. Capital reigns supreme, supply and demand serves as the mechanism for who gets what, and success is measured in productivity levels and net income. The gurus of capital are the corporate chieftains and its acolytes are the advocates of Total Quality Management (TQM). The prevailing mind set is: If something is not measurable, then it lacks value. It was only a matter of time before this ideology and it proponents began wrestling control of the academy.[19]

Needless to say, such views did not mesh well with the goals of the Pataki administration, the Pataki-appointed SUNY trustees, or with the corporate forces arrayed within organizations such as Change, New York. These forces articulated a set of "culture wars" tactics with strategies to shrink public institutions and align their practices with business priorities—exactly as Bowen described in 2001—with no apologies. Ed Sullivan, a member of the state assembly and chair of the higher education committee in 1997, summarized Change, New York and the Pataki administration's two agendas with stark clarity:

Putting in place a tightly drawn conservative curriculum throughout SUNY and reducing the university to a training school that prepares workers for jobs the corporate sector tells us they need.[20]

This vision of the public university as a kind of factory, churning out workers with adequate vocational skills but narrow intellectual horizons and low expectations, contrasted with a range of other liberal, progressive, and radical visions of public higher education as preparation for critical citizenship—teaching students to assess the history of humanity's broadest visions for collective public life, and to then judge for themselves the agendas of politicians. Of course, the Pataki administration's attempt to shrink the democratic goals of public life were not unique to New York, but operated state by state, at the national level, and globally as various forces merged and cooperated under changing conditions.[21]

But when and how did the alignment of economic, political, and cultural agendas operating during the attack on the "Revolting Behavior" conference originate and operate? The first shifts in economic and political alignments occurred in the 1970s, when U.S. based corporations felt squeezed by growing global competition, and profit rates started to tumble precipitously. Though different economic sectors faced different challenges at different moments, 1973 proved to be a turning point overall for the U.S. economy as the percentage of capital raised from lenders began consistently to exceed the percentage from profits. As whole chunks of the world market were lost to foreign enterprises, previously warring domestic business factions converged in a search for ways to buttress sliding profits. Large corporations that had previously supported the New Deal coalition, often cooperating with unions to create relatively secure, higher wage jobs for skilled white male workers, began to see common cause with smaller antiunion, low-wage businesses. Many businesses began to search for ways to reduce labor costs; they moved production units to locations with lower wages and fewer health and safety regulations, inciting competition among U.S. states and localities, and between the U.S. and other nations around the globe, to attract businesses, jobs, and revenue. In addition, a consensus emerged in business circles in favor of curtailing the proportion of earnings contributed to government functions and services.

Cutting taxes, disciplining labor to reduce its costs, and creating an environment friendly to capital accumulation emerged as the most important business priorities during the 1970s. These goals required government action, as well as inaction in crucial areas. They required the dismantling of the New Deal, Great Society coalition of business interests, organized labor, and government activism. This coalition had worked to stabilize social conditions for the worldwide expansion of U.S.-based capitalist enterprises since World War II, as well as to provide some downward redistribution of wealth through government programs and services.[22]

From the New Deal through the Great Society, this form of social democracy in the U.S. was sharply limited and riddled with exclusions. Challenges to the inequitable and undemocratic structures of capitalism were defused and appropriated, or marginalized and contained. But within such sharp limits, economic inequalities were reduced, and democratic participation unevenly expanded. By the 1960s, two decades of growing U.S. domination of the global economy supported a politics of domestic prosperity that infused the demands of social movements for more equitable sharing of wealth, political power, and cultural resources, both within and outside the United States. Business activism in the 1970s attacked the politics of prosperity and downward redistribution with a counterpolitics of scarcity and competition for resources. Rather than support the idea that resources were adequate for broad-based public sharing of the fruits of prosperity, business activists promoted the idea that resources were scarce, and fierce competition among groups and individuals would be required to secure a comfortable life.

Moving from economic motives to effective political mobilizations is always a complex, contingent, and unstable project. Activism and accident collide around issues and circumstances to produce provisional alliances and unintended results, as often as clarity of purpose moves unified groups toward stated goals. Long-standing inequalities, in economic, political, and cultural life, shape possibilities and outcomes but do not determine them. During the 1970s, one particular collision of activism and accident produced a highly influential model for politics in the following decades—the tax revolt behind the passing of Proposition 13 in California during 1978.

Years of organizing to protest regressive property taxes, in California and elsewhere, remained unsuccessful until the highly publicized success of Proposition 13. As recounted by Clarence Lo in *Small Property versus Big Government*,[23] the successful California campaign began in middle income suburban communities, framed primarily as a consumer movement. The California real estate boom produced steep increases in property taxes that homeowners were unable to alter through informal political means. As Lo persuasively argues, homeowners argued for better services and regulations to constrain economic growth as well as for lower taxes—they might have been organized by progressive political forces, perhaps by Ralph Nader. There were in fact some efforts on the left to organize for lower taxes for homeowners and renters, but higher taxes for business.

Despite the potential for an effort on behalf of more progressive property taxes, the late entry into the campaign of more affluent homeowners and community business leaders shaped the movement in the reverse direction, while also ensuring its success. When antitax leader Howard Jarvis unveiled the petition that became Proposition 13, it provided most of the tax relief for businesses rather than homeowners (approximately two-thirds for business, one-third for homeowners, and none for renters). Then when the antitax movement nationalized after 1978, it became a significant launching pad for antistate business conservatism.

Why would consumer/homeowners supportive of government services and regulations sign onto a petition giving most of the tax relief benefits to business? And why would the alliances built during the campaign for Proposition 13 translate into a national coalition for downsizing government and deregulating economic growth? The answers cannot be found in the *economic* interests at stake, which were conflicting between

middle income and affluent homeowners, and among renters, homeowners and small and large businesses. The answers lie in the *politics*
and *cultures of race.*[24]

The long history of racism in the U.S. shaped patterns of residential
racial segregation during the post–World War II period—patterns ex-
acerbated by the accelerating process of racialized suburbanization cir-
cling cities across the country. "White flight" from inner cities into
suburbs was supported by a vast array of government supports and subsidies—from highway construction to federally guaranteed mortgages
(allocated disproportionately to white homebuyers). This expanded
spatialization of racial difference profoundly affected the relationship
of homeowners and businesses to property taxes. This category of
taxation, tied specifically to local geographies of property ownership,
could most easily be imagined as "belonging" to localities, and as constituting a kind of direct payment for local government services. In this
context, many homeowners began to see themselves as consumers of
government, expecting the best return for the price paid in taxes, rather
than as citizens supporting an expansive array of broadly accessible
public agencies and institutions. And this consumer citizenship was
economically and racially differentiated—according to housing patterns—with racial difference dominating shifting conceptions of taxpayers vs. taxeaters, those who paid the bill, and those who siphoned off
the funds of suburban property taxes to support inner city services.

The tax revolt in California, and the subsequent national antitax
movement, rode forward on the racial codings embedded in the economics and spatial distribution of property ownership. Suburban taxpayer citizens imagined themselves in direct competition with city
welfare recipients for government services, a competition covertly
conceived as a zero sum battle of white neighborhoods versus black
and Latino housing projects. This highly distorted imagining—white
homeowners were the recipients of historically high levels of government subsidies during this period (including government-subsidized
mortgages, more easily available to white homeowners than to others)—allowed suburbanites to identify with the "haves," regardless of

actual position in the economic hierarchy—"haves" with something to lose, specifically "their" tax dollars, which were in danger of being redistributed downward along racial lines.[25]

Thus the racial codings of the tax revolt shaped an otherwise strange alliance of homeowners who supported government services and regulations, at least within their "own" localities, with businesses who increasingly opposed them. The politics of the tax revolt shaped a culture supportive of strategies of upward redistribution of wealth, through a process of white homeowner disidentification with racial others—black and Latino city dwellers imagined to exist in a socially disordered, politically isolated, and economically depleting culture of downward redistribution.

The process of coalition building underlying the success of the tax revolt was not a top down conspiracy. Big business originally opposed Proposition 13, in part out of fear that homeowner activism might promote antibusiness rhetoric as well as antistate fervor. National business groups, pro-business politicians, and right-wing activists picked up and ran with the rhetorical strategies and political positionings of the tax revolt only *after* the success of Proposition 13, in its pro-business form. Other local and state level insurgencies, shaped by the politics of racial othering, converged at the national level with more top down, orchestrated campaigns to produce new "conservative" alliances joining politically unstable populist politics with the emerging neoliberal agenda of newly converging business factions. Some of these alliances are documented in Jean Stefanic and Richard Delgado's *No Mercy*, which traces a series of interconnected, race-based, issue-driven campaigns that worked to combine local racist populism with elite agendas, with significant support from conservative/ libertarian/ neoliberal think tanks and foundations: the drive to make English the official language; the coalition supporting restrictions on immigrants contained in Proposition 187 in California; the promotion of racist pseudoscience on race, IQ, and genetics; the attack on affirmative action; the attack on welfare, and the campus culture wars.[26]

Racial politics became the most significant wedge in the dismantling of alliances advocating downward redistribution of economic, political, and cultural resources during the 1970s and 1980s. This focus was a legacy of historic racism, but also directly reflected the power of the Civil Rights movement as a culture of downward redistribution during the previous decade, a power that became more threatening as antiracist politics moved leftward during the 1960s. But the divisions of gender and sexuality were fully exploited as well. Attacks on feminism, on women's reproductive rights, on sexual "permissiveness" and "perversion," both coded and explicit, generated from below as well as from above, multiplied during this period. The full range of this identity politics on the right was brought to bear in support of the core issue of neoliberal policy priorities—welfare "reform."[27]

The campus "culture wars" of the 1980s and 1990s drew on the repertoire of rhetorics and alliances developed since the 1970s, positioning "liberals" and progressives in colleges and universities as simultaneously "elitist" and "alien," in populist mode, and as sucking up taxpayer dollars to support cultures of downward redistribution—multiculturalism, Marxism, "theory," and feminism particularly.[28] Sex panic strategies, honed and perfected during the arts censorship battles and the antigay referenda campaigns of the 1980s and 1990s, played a crucial role as well. Highlighting sexual content helped to frame progressive academic enterprises as simultaneously "too political" and "too personal" for the classroom or campus life—both too confrontational and threatening *as* public debate, and too ridiculous, trivial and inappropriate *for* public institutions.

The orchestrated attack on the "Revolting Behavior" conference at SUNY New Paltz was organized directly from the guidelines developed during the culture wars. An intellectually bankrupt women's studies program sucking tax dollars for a carnival of sexual perversion—this image was perfected for the purpose of discrediting and thus reorganizing the state university system. Appealing to a manufactured grassroots, populist disgust for a frivolous, "liberal" professorate with too much money and time to waste, de Russy and Change, New York sought to persuade a statewide public that strongly supported public education that *this* education was a misuse of *their* money—because it ended up in the pockets of sexual perverts. Combined with racially coded attacks on CUNY (including attacks on ethnic studies programs as well as snide dismissals of wasted spending for "lazy," "ill-prepared," or nonnative English-speaking students), this strategy helped legitimate the precipitous decline in funding and the increasingly centralized control of public higher education in New York. Institutions that housed and incubated a range of cultures of downward redistribution were both downsized and restructured during the late 1990s, with an eye to converting them into corporate resources.[29]

This effort to corporatize the public university system has not been entirely successful—resistance has been strong and sometimes effective. But such resistance is undermined and limited by narrow political frameworks—by simple defenses of academic freedom or specific support for particular programs, departments, professors, courses, and conferences. Effective resistance to the culture war strategy of neoliberal economic, political, and cultural restructuring requires a vision of the significant links among various cultures of downward redistribution in a context of multiple, overlapping inequalities. The women's studies program at SUNY New Paltz offered resources to students and community groups regularly excluded and stigmatized in public life; they also nurtured critiques of the corporatization of the university. For this they were attacked, and the attack had wide political impact. Only a response that exposed the links in the chain of attack from culture to politics to economics, and that forged its own links, operating to stimulate the flow of resources in the opposite direction, might have succeeded—not only in defusing the specific attack, but in building a sustainable progressive opposition. A sustainable opposition would need to connect culture, politics, and economics; identity politics and class politics; universalist rhetoric and particular issues and interests; intellectual and material resources.

Attacks on public higher education in New York, and in the United States more broadly, aimed to *privatize* education by reducing the overall proportion of public funds supporting higher education and by redesigning college and university curricula to more directly serve private business needs. Neoliberal campaigns to downsize public education also aimed to largely abolish the public nature of support for broad-based access to knowledge and information, and to define education more as a matter of *personal responsibility*—a private, primarily economic matter. An effective response, and defense of mass education for democracy, would need to comprehend the overall cultural projects of neoliberalism and their relation to the economic policies and politics that underwrite them.

There is nothing stable or inevitable in the alliances supporting neoliberal agendas, in the U.S. and globally. The alliances linking neoliberal global economics, conservative and right-wing domestic politics, and the culture wars, are provisional—and by the new millennium, fading. Like populist campaigns, the "identity politics" targeted by conservative/neoliberals in the culture wars encompassed a variety of potential and actual political valences, from left to right, from support for upward redistributions of various kinds to impassioned advocacy of downward redistribution. The culture wars strategy allowed emerging neoliberal forces to attack and isolate the cultures of downward redistribution located within social movements since the 1960s. The flip side of this strategy was the nurturing of forms of "identity politics" recruitable for policies of upward redistribution. The culture wars were an effective game plan, but by the 1990s they had become a residual strategy for neoliberals, who could increasingly afford to drop their right wing of religious moralists—a rump formation for an ascendant mainstream neoliberalism. Neoliberalism's emergent strategy for the new millennium: A new "equality" politics compatible with a corporate world order.

3

Equality, Inc.

Immediately after the attacks on the World Trade Towers and the Pentagon on September 11, 2001, Moral Majority founder Rev. Jerry Falwell appeared on the daily broadcast of Rev. Pat Robertson's conservative Christian television show *The 700 Club* to comment on the causes of this tragic violence. Falwell opined that,

> I really believe that the pagans, and the abortionists, and the feminists, and the gays and the lesbians who are actively trying to make that an alternative lifestyle, the ACLU, People for the American Way, all of them who have tried to secularize America, I point the finger in their face and say "you helped this happen."

Falwell went on to claim that, given this national moral state, America "probably deserves" the punishment of terrorism inflicted by God. This typical "culture wars" jeremiad was soon followed by announcements that the relief funds for families of those killed in the World Trade Towers would exclude same-sex domestic partners.[1]

Such attacks and exclusions had been typical fare in national politics since the early 1980s, often implicitly supported or at least tolerated by Republican politicians. But in September 2001, Falwell's statement was quickly repudiated by a lineup of politicians from both major national parties, and the exclusion of same-sex domestic partners from government supported relief funds for families of 9/11 victims was rescinded by the Republican president George W. Bush and the Republican governor of New York, George Pataki, who commented that,

In all honesty, for too long, the party that I am proud to be a member of... was a party that did express intolerance.[2]

Many pundits noted that the national tragedy of 9/11 seemed to change the climate of "official" opinion, with regard to lesbian and gay Americans in particular, toward greater acceptance. But greater acceptance of the most assimilated, gender-appropriate, politically mainstream portions of the gay population had already occurred—in politics, media representations, and the workplace—since the mid-1990s especially.[3] Neoliberal politicians and corporate employers and media in the United States had already moved significantly in the direction of "diversity," if not toward substantive equality. From the Clinton administration's serious efforts to recruit racial minorities and women into high level government service, and to reduce the range of exclusions of sexual minorities, to the G. W. Bush administration's more clearly token gestures of inclusion, the rhetoric of "official" neoliberal politics shifted during the 1990s from "culture wars" alliances, to a superficial "multiculturalism" compatible with the global aspirations of U.S. business interests.[4] "Culture wars" attacks and alliances did not disappear, but they receded from the national political stage in favor of an emergent rhetorical commitment to diversity, and to a narrow, formal, nonredistributive form of "equality" politics for the new millennium.

Along with this move toward "multicultural" diversity within the neoliberal mainstream, some proponents of "equality politics" moved away from the civil rights lobbies and identity politics organizations to advocate the abandonment of progressive-left affiliations, and the adoption of a neoliberal brand of identity/equality politics. These organizations, activists, and writers promote "color-blind" anti–affirmative action racial politics, conservative-libertarian "equality feminism," and gay "normality." They are currently a relatively small, emergent minority—but a highly visible new formation within neoliberal politics.[5] If they succeed in wresting the constituencies for identity politics further away from the progressive-left, enfolding a larger proportion of these populations within neoliberal alliances, the result would be a major realignment in U.S. politics. Such a realignment would rival the 1970s' "southern strategy" that moved phalanxes of formerly Democratic voters out of the New Deal coalition and into the Republican columns, largely through "culture wars" racism.[6] Such a realignment, though still only an unlikely possibility, would further shrink and marginalize the progressive-left—a danger only amplified by the left's own failures to fully integrate identity and cultural politics.

This chapter provides a case study in this newly emergent neoliberal "equality" politics drawn from the lesbian and gay rights movement. National lesbian and gay civil rights, lobbying and litigation organizations have nearly all moved away from constituency mobilization and community-based consultation during the past decade. Following the national political culture to the right, and pressed by the exigencies of fundraising for survival, gay civil rights groups have adopted neoliberal rhetoric and corporate decision-making models. No longer representative of a broad-based progressive movement, many of the dominant national lesbian and gay civil rights organizations have become the lobbying, legal, and public relations firms for an increasingly narrow gay, moneyed elite. Consequently, the push for gay marriage and military service has replaced the array of political, cultural, and economic issues that galvanized the national groups as they first emerged from a progressive social movement context several decades earlier.[7]

The Human Rights Campaign (HRC), for instance—the richest national gay and lesbian civil rights lobby in Washington, D.C.—inaugurated the new millennium with a march on Washington. Promoted as the successor to many previous such national mobilizations, the Millennium March actually broke decisively with the history of gay movement organizing in the United States. Brought to you by corporate sponsors corralled by a corporate-style board of directors with little outside input, the Millennium March was more of a public relations media campaign than a grassroots action.[8] Community organizers nationwide protested the top-down corporate planning process and the Benetton-ad style of "diversity" politics that the march deployed. The protestors built on the outrage generated by HRC just two years earlier when its board endorsed antiabortion Republican Al D'Amato over liberal-centrist Democrat Charles Schumer for a New York Senate seat.

Since September 11, 2001, this rightward drift toward neoliberal politics has intensified, with an added emphasis on the Americanism of model gay "heroes" and "victims" as a rhetorical boost for demands for inclusion in marriage and the military. The potential for jingoistic blindness in this moment was starkly illustrated when the National Coalition of Anti-Violence Programs responded to an instance of homophobia that occurred early in the U.S. bombing of Afghanistan during fall 2001. An Associated Press photograph of a bomb being loaded onto the USS *Enterprise* showed a warhead emblazoned with the dare, "Hijack this Fags." The antiviolence projects protested in a press release,

> The message equates gays with the "enemy," it places gay, lesbian and bisexual servicemembers, who are serving as honorably as anyone else at this time at risk and dishonors them.... The warhead on the USS Enterprise is as contemptible and a far more serious instance of gay-bashing because it comes from those charged with our protection and defense.[9]

New York activist Bill Dobbs commented in reply,

> Yes, the graffiti in question is deplorable. But then there is the slight matter of the bomb itself. And what happens when it is armed, dropped from the air and explodes. Does the National Coalition of Anti-Violence Programs (a coalition of gay groups) speak to such matters? Surely "violence" is implicated in this setting. While many Americans raise questions about the current military campaign— amidst reports of civilian casualties—NCVAP avoids any messy policy issues and sends the message that the bombs and the dropping of same is fine. As long as there is no bad graffiti on them. Given

this sort of Gay Tunnel Vision, I wonder if NCVAP would put out a laudatory statement if the missions had gay/lesbian/bisexual/transgender bombardier(s).[10]

The Human Rights Campaign and the National Coalition of Anti-Violence Programs have not been alone in developing versions of such blinkered political vision. Often misunderstood and criticized by progressive activists as single issue politics—thus the tag "gay tunnel vision"—national gay civil rights politics in the new millennium is actually developing as the "gay equality" branch of multi-issue neoliberalism.

Another example: At the 1999 "Liberty for All" Log Cabin National Leadership Conference in New York, assembled gay Republicans from across the U.S. heard a keynote address from then New York City mayor Rudolph Giuliani, and a series of plenary lectures from Winnie Stachelberg of the Human Rights Campaign, Brian Bond of the Gay and Lesbian Victory Fund, Jonathan Rauch of the *National Journal*, and Urvashi Vaid, director of the National Gay and Lesbian Task Force Policy Institute. From her plenary platform, Vaid called for real dialogue, mutual respect, and even affinity between gay groups and gay leaders at serious political odds, against a backdrop of community unity.

But the conference sponsors were only superficially receptive to Vaid's call for respectful, inclusive dialogue. Rich Tafel, executive director of the Log Cabin Republicans, expressed a different notion of the basis for gay political unity—a transformed movement with a new center and definite exclusions:

> The conference was the most important we've ever held, and its success solidified a clear shift that is taking place in the gay movement. There is a transformation going on across the country. . . . And [as] with any such transformation, those who had the most invested in the polarized status quo, notably extremists on the far left and far right, are beginning to resort to increasingly desperate tactics to stop it.[11]

At the conference, Jonathan Rauch named that new center as "libertarian radical independent" and pointed to the online writers' group, the
Independent Gay Forum (IGF), as the "cutting edge" of a new gay
movement.

Under the banner "Forging a Gay Mainstream," the IGF Web site
proclaims the organization's principles:

- We support the full inclusion of gays and lesbians in civil society
  with legal equality and equal social respect. We argue that gays
  and lesbians, in turn, contribute to the creativity, robustness, and
  decency of our national life.
- We share a belief in the fundamental virtues of the American
  system and its traditions of individual liberty, personal moral
  autonomy and responsibility, and equality before the law. We
  believe those traditions depend on the institutions of a market
  economy, free discussion, and limited government.
- We deny "conservative" claims that gays and lesbians pose any
  threat to social morality or the political order.
- We equally oppose "progressive" claims that gays should support
  radical social change or restructuring of society.
- We share an approach, but we disagree on many particulars. We
  include libertarians, moderates, and classical liberals. We hold
  differing views on the role of government, personal morality, religious faith, and personal relationships. We share these disagree-
  ments openly: we hope that readers will find them interesting and
  thought provoking.[12]

This variety of "third way" rhetoric is central to post-1990 neoliberalism (see chapter 1). The Independent Gay Forum follows this
format, positioning itself against antigay conservatism and queer
progressive politics—between which poles the "differing views" of its
listed writers may range. Among the thirty men and three women
named on the Web site (all white, with the exception of one African-
American man) are well-known writers like Andrew Sullivan, author of

Virtually Normal: An Argument About Homosexuality (Knopf, 1995), and Bruce Bawer, author of *A Place at the Table: The Gay Individual in American Society* (Poseidon Press, 1993), as well as somewhat more obscure figures such as Walter Olson, a columnist for the magazine *Reason* and author of *The Excuse Factory: How Employment Law Is Paralyzing the American Workplace* (Free Press, 1997), and David Boaz, executive vice president of the libertarian Cato Institute and author of *Libertarianism: A Primer* (Free Press, 1997). Also included are a few popular writers with more murkily centrist views like Eric Marcus, coauthor with Greg Louganis of *Breaking the Surface* (Random House, 1995) and a handful of academically trained intellectuals, such as sociologist Stephen O. Murray, author of *American Gay* (University of Chicago Press, 1996).

On the surface the IGF Web site's collection of downloadable articles is targeted at conservative moralists, antigay church doctrine, and ex-gay propaganda on the one hand (Paul Varnell's "Changing Churches" and "The Ex-Gay Pop-Gun"), and at queer cultural and intellectual radicalism on the other (Stephen O. Murray's "Why I Don't Take Queer Theory Seriously" and Jennifer Vanasco's "Queer Dominance Syndrome"). But surrounding and shaping the familiar political triangulation, and the repeated assimilationist tirades against more flamboyant in-your-face gay activists, is a broader agenda for the future of democracy. This highly visible and influential center-libertarian-conservative-classical liberal formation in gay politics aims to contest and displace the expansively democratic vision represented by progressive activists such as Urvashi Vaid, replacing it with a model of a narrowly constrained public life cordoned off from the "private" control and vast inequalities of economic life. This new formation is not merely a position on the spectrum of gay movement politics, but is a crucial new part of the cultural front of neoliberalism in the United States.

By producing gay equality rhetoric and lobbying for specific policies that work within the framework of neoliberal politics generally, the IGF and its affiliated writers hope to (1) shore up the strength of neoliberalism in relation to its critics on the right and left, but especially in relation to the gay left, becoming what journalist Richard Goldstein has called antiprogressive-left "attack queers,"[13] and (2) push the neoliberal consensus in the direction of their brand of libertarian/moderate/conservative gay politics and away from politically attractive antigay alternatives.

The beachhead established by the writers now posted on the IGF site has been remarkably effective in creating what Michael Warner has called "a virtual gay movement" in the mainstream and gay press since the mid-1990s.[14] By invoking a phantom mainstream public of "conventional" gays who represent the responsible center, these writers have worked to position "liberationists" and leftists as irresponsible "extremists" or as simply anachronistic (in this way, they echo the efforts of right-wing talk-radio hosts, conservative television news commentators, and many mainstream neoliberal politicians to smear all opinion to the left of them as "extreme" or "old-fashioned"). But this group has been much less successful in influencing national policy; they have failed to persuade many mainstream politicians to support their core issues of full gay access to marriage and military service. But they are certainly not yet defeated on these issues or in their overall project of providing a new sexual politics for neoliberalism in the new millennium.

The new neoliberal sexual politics of the IGF might be termed *the new homonormativity*—it is a politics that does not contest dominant heteronormative assumptions and institutions, but upholds and sustains them, while promising the possibility of a demobilized gay constituency and a privatized, depoliticized gay culture anchored in domesticity and consumption.[15] IGF writers produce this politics through a double-voiced address to an imagined gay public, on the one hand, and to the national mainstream constructed by neoliberalism on the other.[16] This address works to bring the desired public into political salience as a perceived mainstream, primarily through a rhetorical remapping of public/private boundaries designed to shrink gay public spheres, and redefine gay equality against the "civil rights agenda" and "liberationism," as access to the institutions of domestic privacy, the "free" market, and patriotism.

Given the history of gay rights activism in the U.S., this remapping is a big job. Though the fight for gay equality has been rocked by internal conflict over assimilationist versus confrontational tactics since the emergence of the homophile movement in the 1950s, the overall goals and directions of change have been relatively consistent: the expansion of a right to sexual privacy against the intrusive, investigatory labeling powers of the state, and the simultaneous expansion of gay public life through institution building and publicity.[17]

During the 1950s and 1960s, homophile movement organizations entered a fraught rhetorical battlefield, riddled with intensely contradictory conflicts over public/private distinctions, and over the "proper" relations of the state, "public" life in civil society, the economy and intimate life. "Conservatives" argued to privatize most of collective life in the U.S., opposing state enforcement of democratic access in the economy and civil society, but *advocating* state regulation of marriage, reproduction, and sexuality. In response, "liberals" pushed for state assurance of broad public access to commercial as well as government institutions, and defended the *privacy* of marital, reproductive, and sexual decisions (see chapter 1). Homophile organizations engaged in these battles with necessarily complex rhetorical and political strategies, attempting to ensure *both* full access to public life, *and* privacy defined strategically as freedom from state-imposed criminalization and stigma.

Homophile movement organizations, including the Mattachine Society, the Janus Society, and the Daughters of Bilitis, and homophile publications from *One*, the *Mattachine Review*, and the *Ladder* to *Drum*, and *The Homosexual Citizen*, served as platforms and forums for radicals like Mattachine founder and Communist Party member Harry Hay and well-known playwright Lorraine Hansberry, cautious and assimilationist reformers including DOB stalwarts Del Martin and Phyllis Lyon, and militant single-issue activists such as Franklin Kameny and Barbara Gittings. But despite internal disputes and significant political shifts over time, the homophile activists intervened in postwar conflicts by steadily expanding the notion of sexual or personal privacy to include, not only sexual relations between consenting adults at home, but freedom from surveillance and entrapment in public, collective settings. They worked in company with an expanding commercial sector serving gay and lesbian constituencies to attack the investigatory activities of the local police, state liquor authorities and the FBI, as well as federal government employers, in public settings including bars and parks as well as workplaces. This complex maneuver involved not only defending the right to privacy of couples at home, but defining a kind of right-to-privacy-in-public—a zone of immunity from state regulation, surveillance, and harassment. This project worked along with efforts to expand the allowable scope of sexual expression in public culture, both commercial and nonprofit/artistic, to complexly remap zones of collective autonomy in ways that displaced the conservative boundaries of corporate freedoms and personal/public moral constraints. The homophile organizations attacked police raids of commercial establishments catering to "open" homosexuals, especially bars, opposed the entrapment of men having sex in public parks or restrooms, and organized against the stigmatizing and firing of "homosexual" state employees. And they invented new rhetorical and political means to do so.[18]

In the 1970s, gay liberation exploded onto a rapidly shifting scene of contest over the meanings of public and private, and the related meanings of democracy and autonomy in collective and personal life. Following the 1969 Stonewall rebellion and the subsequent emergence of new organizations and rhetorics, gay politics began to interact intensely with feminist, countercultural, and antiracist rhetorics and strategies. The emphasis of political activism shifted away from arguments for privacy as autonomy, and toward public visibility and publicity. But the work of recombining rhetorics of public and private was not abandoned; the project of building an unmolested collective life required continuing remappings of a right-to-privacy-in-public, and a right to publicize "private" matters considered offensive to the phantom "general public."

By the 1980s, antigay forces had retooled their strategies. They began slowly and unevenly to concede a right to privacy, but they defined privacy as a kind of confinement, a cordon sanitaire protecting "public" sensibilities. They attacked gay rhetorical claims for privacy-in-public and for publicizing the private, specifically, and worked to define the private sphere as an isolated, domestic site completely out of range of any public venue. Thus the strategy of state No Promo Homo referenda and attacks on public funding for homoerotic art—gay sex is fine in "private" but should not be "displayed" or "promoted" in public. Meanwhile AIDS activism deepened and expanded the scope of gay politics, crucially supplementing a newly well-established gay rights movement focused on antidiscrimination and decriminalization. New activist energies organized in the face of the AIDS pandemic also helped to spawn a vigorous, emergent queer political front with visions of social and cultural transformation beyond the limits of identity politics.[19]

By the 1992 presidential contest that elected Bill Clinton, neoliberal organizations and politicians had begun the task of separating themselves from the moral conservatism of the religious right, as well as from the "failed" policies of "old" tax-and-spend liberals. And alongside radical and progressive AIDS activism, a new strain of gay moralism appeared—attacks on "promiscuity" and the "gay lifestyle" accompanied advocacy of monogamous marriage as a responsible disease prevention strategy.[20] In this fertile ground, the coterie of writers attached to the Independent Gay Forum began to spread the word about their new gay politics—a politics that offers a dramatically shrunken public sphere and a narrow zone of "responsible" domestic privacy.

The authors and articles collected on the IGF Web site are generally glib; the arguments assembled are characterized more by put downs, pleas and polemics than by sustained argument or analysis. One of the best known writers exemplifying this approach on the site is Bruce Bawer, self-described elitist and monogamous churchgoing Christian, former writer for the right-wing *American Spectator*, editor of an anthology of articles by IGF colleagues, *Beyond Queer: Challenging Gay Left Orthodoxy*, and author of a long list of essays and reviews as well as of his own thoroughly humorless little homily, *A Place at the Table: The Gay Individual in American Society*. Bawer is practiced at the rhetorical techniques of triangulation, as well as the less subtle joys of naked left bashing. He invokes "most gay people" as a Nixonian "silent majority" of the conventional opposed to left "queerthink." He describes his own and his wished-for constituency's views as "postideological," and positions them in relation to the "anachronistic" multi-issue progressive politics of the Stonewall generation.[21] In two of his shorter screeds, he takes special aim at Urvashi Vaid, positioning her well outside the new center of the IGF's gay public by calling her an "ideological extremist" whose rhetoric is "old." He goes well beyond simple left-bashing, though, to set forth his alternative vision of the best sources of social change for gay equality, arguing that,

> In 1995, even as veteran activist Urvashi Vaid issued a call for a radical gay rights movement aligned with workers and other victim groups against the capitalist oppressor, mounting evidence suggested that major corporations may well do more to bring about gay equality than any other Establishment institution (or, for that matter, the National Gay and Lesbian Task Force).... More than ever, it seemed reasonable to suggest that much of gay America's hope resides not in working-class revolt but in its exact opposite— a trickling down of gay-positive sentiments from elite corporate boardrooms into shops, farms, and factories.[22]

Bawer looks unabashedly to a trickle down vision of equality as corporate largess, and gleefully anticipates the Disneyfication of democracy as boardroom dealmaking.

As basic left-bashing, though, Bawer's attacks on Vaid have been mild and inconsequential compared with the efforts of IGF writer Rob Blanchard (now deceased) and his associates in San Antonio, Texas, who joined with Christian right forces to attack the reputation and funding of the progressive, lesbian-of-color led arts and community organization, the Esperanza Peace and Justice Center. In 1997, Blanchard and five other white gay men claiming affiliation with the National Lesbian and Gay Journalists Association, the San Antonio Equal Rights Political Caucus, the Log Cabin Republicans, and the San Antonio Gay and Lesbian Community Center, signed a letter to the city's mayor and city council members asking that Esperanza be denied city funding, arguing that,

> it is a political organization—obsessed with victimhood and using "sexism, racism, classism, and homophobia" as rhetorical and political ploys to extract guilt money from individuals and organizations, including the City. Esperanza has made its battle for tax dollars a referendum on homosexuality and we resent this. But Esperanza's greatest damage to the gay and lesbian community is the divisiveness it creates within by repeatedly injecting issues of class, race and gender for self-serving purposes.[23]

This attack attributes "divisiveness" to an inclusive agenda, and locates unity in the unmarked centrality of prosperous white men, whose interests unproblematically define the interests of "the gay and lesbian community." It goes further to participate aggressively in the right-wing strategy of denying public funding for "political" arts projects. Neoliberal advocacy, of course, is defined as the nonpolitical exclusion of "issues of class, race and gender."

Such attacks, while both ugly and revealing, don't clearly illuminate the underlying political logic of the IGF's new gay paradigm. The writer whose work most fully elaborates an overarching framework for the efforts of this group is former *New Republic* editor Andrew Sullivan, a prolific essayist with a Ph.D. in political science from Harvard and analytic aspirations somewhat higher than the level of earnest exhortation, vituperative attack, or clever polemics.

Well, Sullivan may aim higher, but in his most widely cited book, *Virtually Normal*, he falls well short of sustained, coherent analysis. He nonetheless sets the terms for neoliberal arguments about sexual politics, beginning with a triangulating framework that attacks the "extremes" of what he calls *prohibitionism* and *liberationism*, and that claims to reconcile the best arguments of contemporary conservatives and liberals to offer, in the "third way" mode, a new approach.

Sullivan's prohibitionism is the kind of social conservatism that would morally condemn and legally punish homosexuality. He distinguishes this view from bigotry, however, and argues respectfully that,

> In an appeal to "nature," the most persuasive form of this argument is rooted in one of the oldest traditions of thought in the West, a tradition that still carries a great deal of intuitive sense. It posits a norm—the heterosexual identity—that is undeniably valuable in any society and any culture, that seems to characterize the vast majority of humanity, and without which civilization would simply evaporate: and it attempts to judge homosexuality by the standards of that norm.[24]

He follows this claim with an extended discussion of the published views of the Roman Catholic Church, from the writings of St. Thomas Aquinas to statements of church dogma on homosexual relations published in 1975 and 1986. The centrality of Catholic doctrine to his analysis, rather than, say, the religious views of Baptists or the political opinions of the Republican Party, is not explained or justified—the fact that Sullivan is himself Catholic seems to be the motivation for this choice. He ultimately rejects the prohibitionist view, even in the respectfully distorted form in which he presents one variant of antigay discourse, as internally inconsistent (nonprocreative heterosexuality would have to be condemned and punished as well as homosexuality in a consistent approach) and just plain wrong in positing homosexuality as a threat to the predominance and prestige of the traditional, heterosexual family. The core of Sullivan's argument here is also key to his entire framework—he argues that homosexuality is an involuntary condition (created by both nature and nurture at a very young age) in

a small fixed minority of the population. In an analogy to natural variation he argues that,

> As albinos remind us of the brilliance of color; as redheads offer a
> startling contrast to the blandness of their peers; as genius teaches
> us, by contrast, of the virtue of moderation: so the homosexual per-
> son might be seen as a natural foil to the heterosexual norm, a vari-
> ation that does not eclipse the theme, but resonates with it.[25]

He implicitly concedes, here and throughout the book, that if homosexuality could be somehow chosen by more people than a very, very
tiny percentage of "waverers," then antigay policies might make sense
as discouragement of this choice. In his view, it is only because homosexuality is involuntary, and therefore cannot threaten an equally involuntary heterosexual majority, that attacking it morally and legally
does not make sense.

Sullivan inveighs against liberationism for a similar reason—its
proponents' insistence that sexual identities are socially constructed,
rather than timelessly fixed within contemporary categories. On his
side here he claims that "history itself," as uncovered by "contemporary historians," concurs with science and psychology in affirming the
presence of homosexuals in all times and places. The fact that the
overwhelming majority of historians of sexuality (several of whom he
names or footnotes in other contexts) make precisely the opposite argument is unmentioned.[26]

But it is not only his historical arguments that are unsupported;
Sullivan's description of what he calls liberationism is completely confused, and finally much more cartoonishly reductive than his description of prohibitionism. For the purpose of ridicule and dismissal, he
collapses virtually all the political and intellectual approaches to sexual
politics on the contemporary radical or progressive-left—approaches
wildly at odds with each other analytically and strategically—into one
big pot labeled "Foucauldean." He includes and collapses militant identity politics, such as Michelangelo Signorile's favored tactic of "outing"

hypocritical closeted gays, or Larry Kramer's plans and pronounce-
ments on AIDS politics, with anti-identity versions of queer coalition
politics (which explicitly reject the parameters of narrow gay identity
politics, like Signorile's and Kramer's), and the writings of academics
from social constructionist historians and sociologists to poststructuralist critics and philosophers, especially Judith Butler.

This hodgepodge of diverse and contentious activists and intellectuals is presented as a monolith of rigid orthodoxies. The strategy of
"outing" is hilariously described as "a classic case of Foucauldean resistance"—though no Foucauldian ever supported it. (The supporters
of outing, prominently including Michelangelo Signorile, were nearly
as hostile to academic writers who quote Michel Foucault as Sullivan
himself—while most Foucault fans were severe critics of this practice.)
"Queer" is described as a uniform and compulsory identity "used to label ... to tell everyone that they have a single and particular identity."
But in fact, "queer" has been used most often precisely to question the
uniformity of sexual identities and to replace a list of relatively fixed
identity categories (like Sullivan's "gay" identity) with a notion of flexible, antinormative, politicized sexualities.[27] And as a final summary
and dismissal Sullivan proclaims,

> The liberationists prefer to concentrate—for where else can they
> go?—on those instruments of power which require no broader con-
> versation, no process of dialogue, no moment of compromise, no
> act of engagement. So they focus on outing, on speech codes, on
> punitive measures against opponents on campuses, on the enforce-
> ment of new forms of language, by censorship and intimidation.[28]

This "authoritarian" project well describes the fantasized enemies of the
right wing/neoliberal alliance in the culture wars, but it bears no relation to the range of policies, projects, and arguments Sullivan tries to
collect under the umbrella "liberationist." While some campus activists support speech codes and some liberal organizations fight for hate
crimes laws, many of the writers Sullivan names have opposed these

specific proposals—his bête noir, Judith Butler, wrote *Excitable Speech* specifically to oppose efforts to regulate speech or belief.[29] But then, coherent analysis and engagement is less the point in Sullivan's discussion of so-called liberationists than it is in his discussion of the Catholic Church. Sullivan is not *addressing* the left, he is caricaturing it.

Sullivan really gets down to business when he turns to classical liberalism, in its contemporary liberal and conservative formations. These are the political perspectives he takes seriously; the ones he hopes to "marry" to derive a new politics of homosexuality. He defines liberalism as the commitment to a formally neutral state, and to the foundational freedoms of action, speech, and choice—most fundamentally expressed in freedom of contract. By this definition, contemporary liberalism has deviated dangerously; in Sullivan's view, this has occurred particularly as a response to the politics of race in the United States.

Sullivan's account of the history of the state in the U.S., and of the background and legacies of progressive liberalism, is severely stunted and distorted—leaving out little details like the role of the turn-of-the-century women's movement, the labor movement, and the New Deal, for instance.[30] But his project is not to get the history right, it is to set up his argument. He wants to position the "civil rights agenda" as *the* wrong road in contemporary liberal politics. And, though he vacillates about whether the historical injustices of race might have justified some departure from the tenets of classical liberalism, he ultimately critiques the Civil Rights movement's legacy of antidiscrimination law and particularly affirmative action, as veering too far away from the proper goals of state neutrality and private freedom of contract. If the politics of homosexuality continues to follow this model, he argues, the state and the law "will be forced into being a mixture of moral education, psychotherapy and absolution. Liberalism was invented specifically to oppose that use of the law."[31]

But when Sullivan turns his attention to contemporary conservatism, he suddenly alters his attitude toward the public inculcation of "values." He mostly endorses what he calls "conservative goods," with the exception of the hypocritical practice of private tolerance coupled with public disapproval of homosexuality. He believes that this conservative public/private pact of discretion is breaking down, even though it still underlies many state policies, including the logic behind the military's "don't ask, don't tell" policy. But he doesn't argue that, in the face of such breakdown, conservative family values should retreat to state neutrality, as he recommends for progressive values of equality and diversity. Instead, he claims to have a plan to offer a new public/private mapping that can combine conservative goods with classical liberal state neutrality.

Sullivan's plan is simple. It involves focusing primarily on two issues—gay access to marriage and the military—then demobilizing the gay population to a "prepolitical" condition.

The beauty of the debate over gays in the military, for Sullivan, is that even though it has temporarily been lost for the forces of gay inclusion, it garnered "the best of both worlds"—it allows the conservative to "point to the virtues of a loyal and dedicated soldier, homosexual or heterosexual, and celebrate his [sic] patriotism," with absolutely no abrogation of liberal principles. The marriage debate provides an even better opportunity. As the proclaimed centerpiece of Sullivan's new politics,

> Marriage is not simply a private contract; it is a social and public recognition of a private commitment. As such, it is the highest public recognition of personal integrity.[32]

But wait! Doesn't this role for marriage sound an awful lot like the dangerous mixture of "moral education, psychotherapy, and absolution" that Sullivan warns progressive liberals against? According to Sullivan's account of liberal principles, should the state be in the business of recognizing one version of "personal integrity"? Apparently so. In comparing support for gay marriage to the currently available alternative government policy, passage of domestic partnership provisions for unmarried couples, Sullivan is the most explicit about the benefits of his plan:

The conservative's worries start with the ease of the relationship. To be sure, domestic partners have to prove financial interdependence, shared living arrangements, and a commitment to mutual caring. But they don't need to have a sexual relationship or even closely mirror old-style marriage. In principle, an elderly woman and her live-in nurse could qualify, or a pair of frat buddies. Left as it is, the concept of domestic partnership could open a Pandora's box of litigation and subjective judicial decision-making about who qualifies....

More important for conservatives, the concept of domestic partnership chips away at the prestige of traditional relationships and undermines the priority we give them.... Marriage provides an anchor, if an arbitrary and often weak one, in the maelstrom of sex and relationships to which we are all prone. It provides a mechanism for emotional stability and economic security. We rig the law in its favor not because we disparage all forms of relationship other than the nuclear family, but because we recognize that not to promote marriage would be to ask too much of human virtue.[33]

One might argue that domestic partnership, as Sullivan describes it, meets the criteria of state neutrality about "values" better than the marriages to which he advocates the state supply prestige. It certainly seems more democratic, less steeped in hierarchy and subjective judgment, more egalitarian about how material and symbolic benefits might be allocated to households—not to mention a better approximation of his vaunted freedom of contract. But Sullivan upholds the most conventional and idealized form of marriage as lifetime monogamy—he says that he has tried to construct for himself the "mirror image of the happy heterosexuality I imagined around me"—in utterly prefeminist terms (the operative word is *imagined*, and clearly from a husbandly point of view).[34]

But Sullivan's support for gay marriage is more than a conservative opinion on a hot button issue—it is a linchpin for his broader political vision, one that overlaps considerably with most of the writers in the IGF panoply. Sullivan aims to construct a new public/private distinction that mobilizes gay equality rhetoric on behalf of a miniaturized state and constricted public life, confined to a very few policy decisions, coupled with a vast zone of "private" life dominated by "voluntary" economic and civic transactions, however conglomerated, oligarchic and unaccountable. Marriage is a strategy for privatizing gay politics and culture for the new neoliberal world order. He explains,

> It is, of course, not the least of the ironies of this politics—and of predominantly political argument—that, in the last resort, its objectives are in some sense not political at all. The family is prior to the state; the military is coincident with it. Heterosexuals would not conceive of such rights as things to be won, but as things that predate modern political discussion. But it says something about the unique status of homosexuals in our society that we now have to be political in order to be prepolitical. Our battle, after all, is not for political victory but for personal integrity. In the same way that many of us had to leave our families in order to join them again, so now as citizens, we have to embrace politics if only ultimately to be free of it.[35]

There is no vision of a collective, democratic public culture, or of an ongoing engagement with contentious cantankerous queer politics. Instead we have been administered a kind of political sedative—we get marriage and the military, then we go home and cook dinner, forever.[36]

Such views have been elaborated on Sullivan's personal Web site in the years following the publication of *Virtually Normal*. Since 9/11, Sullivan's writings have emphasized masculinist American nationalism, as well as intensified left-bashing. He posted praise for the virile masculinity of 9/11 "heroes" such as gay rugby player Mark Bingham, one of the passengers who downed an American Airlines flight over Pennsylvania rather than allow hijackers to commandeer it, and Father Mychal

Judge, the gay priest who ministered to fallen firefighters near the World Trade Towers sight. For instance, in supposedly calling for increased acceptance of both gay men and lesbians, Sullivan wrote,

> And perhaps the rugby players and jocks will take a minute to remember Mark Bingham, a national hero who was also gay, and reassess some attitudes toward gay men and women in sports. Perhaps they will also readjust some prejudice that still sees gay men as weak, ineffectual or cowardly. Nothing could be further from the truth. And when the Church celebrates a man like Father Mychal, a gay man who was loved in a surpassingly male and masculine world, perhaps they will also ask themselves to rethink the pain and heartache and cruelty they have inflicted on so many gay men and women, people who have served the Church as deeply as anyone in history.[37]

This sexism, and positive regard for all things "masculine," was supplemented by overt misogyny in Sullivan's New York Public Library lecture of June 7, 2001, "The Emasculation of Gay Politics." There he blamed "New Left feminism" for taking over gay organizations and institutions, driving gay men into alienated exclusion. This kind of masculinist politics is of a piece with Sullivan's neoliberalism: He advocates a shrunken state, expanded commercial "freedoms" from democratic accountability, a civil society riven with exclusions, and a privatized, gendered, hierarchical family. He only asks that gays be allowed to exist within this neoliberal landscape, so long as they support sentimental masculinist nationalism and challenge nothing.[38]

Sullivan is probably the single most influential writer among the neoliberal gang of gays, published in a wide range of mainstream and gay newspapers and periodicals. But he is certainly not the sole voice along the range of moderate Democrats and Republicans to radical right wing libertarians in the mix. The Liberty Education Forum, an offshoot of the Log Cabin Republicans, also promotes this range of "new" gay voices.[39] Libertarians are particularly voluble; the IGF Web site probably adapted its name from the rightist libertarian Independent Women's Forum and its brand of neoliberal "equality feminism."[40] One might imagine that, in the more libertarian environs of such politics, one might find more of a deregulating fervor in relation to intimate life. But no, opposition to state administration of marriage among gay libertarians, other than among the left wing variety, is rare. But so is the kind of sentimentality and sanctimoniousness that is rife in discussions like Sullivan's. More typical of libertarian thinking is the hard-edged argumentation of David Boaz, the Cato Institute vice president.

Boaz argues, like Sullivan, that gay marriage is preferable to domestic partnership, because the latter undermines marriage's premium on commitment. But Boaz is much more explicit about the economic role of marriage and its relation to the "free" market—both impose discipline and privatize dependency among the poor. In "Reviving the Inner City," Boaz argues in fine libertarian feather against drug laws as well as against welfare state programs as "plantations" for blacks. But he makes clear that the problem is ultimately that welfare programs offer resources especially to poor women, who are enabled to make undesirable choices. The combination of market discipline, in the form of dependency on low-wage jobs, and family discipline, in the form of dependency on husbands, operate together to create the best environment for Boaz's ideal world:

> The stark truth is that as long as the welfare state makes it possible for young women to have children without a husband and to survive without a job, the inner city will continue to be marked by poverty, crime and despair.[41]

Here Boaz, like Sullivan, reveals his neoliberal vision—though without the sentimentality. Boaz is clear in arguing that the family is a gendered institution for privatizing social costs—women, dependent on husbands or the low-wage job market, must bear responsibility for child care costs (and elder and extended family care costs), and provide domestic labor. He is equally as clear that the state must refrain from interfering in the "free" market or in the biases and brutalities of discriminatory civic institutions. But he does not advocate that the state refrain from regulating family life through marriage laws—he simply asks that gay people be included, without any accompanying critical revisions. Like nearly all the writers on the IGF Web site, Boaz and Sullivan both argue for *privatization* and *personal responsibility* as means for transferring costs from the corporate taxes, paid to the state and dispensed as social service programs, to the family and civil society, where women's unpaid labor absorbs the lion's share of the burden.

This kind of political vision ultimately displaces any belief that Urvashi Vaid or other progressive activists might have that "the gay movement" is one big tent of advocacy for generally democratic and egalitarian goals, with variation from single-issue focuses and assimilationist styles and strategies to multi-issue coalitionism and confrontational tactics. Arguably, such a description may accurately represent the organized gay movement from homophile activism in the 1950s and 1960s, through lesbian feminism and gay liberation in the 1970s, to liberal gay rights advocacy in the 1980s. But since the 1990s, the influential new gay politics of the Independent Gay Forum writers have marked a decisive break from the centrist liberal/progressive to radical left continuum generally invoked by the phrase "the gay movement."

This gay right wing, self-constituted as a new center, is definitively *not* a single-issue political lobby. The IGF's gay equality rhetoric is a proffered new window-dressing for a broad, multi-issue neoliberal politics. The privacy-in-public claims and publicizing strategies of "the gay movement" are rejected in favor of public recognition of a domesticated, depoliticized privacy. The democratic diversity of proliferating forms of sexual dissidence is rejected in favor of the naturalized variation of a fixed minority arrayed around a state-endorsed heterosexual primacy and prestige. This new homonormativity comes equipped with a rhetorical recoding of key terms in the history of gay politics: "equality" becomes narrow, formal access to a few conservatizing institutions, "freedom" becomes impunity for bigotry and vast inequalities in commercial life and civil society, the "right to privacy" becomes domestic confinement, and democratic politics itself becomes something to be escaped. All of this adds up to a corporate culture managed by a minimal state, achieved by the neoliberal privatization of affective as well as economic and public life.

Welcome to the New World Order! Coming soon to a mainstream near you....

4

Love *and* Money

During the 1990s, neoliberal politics and policies enjoyed years of breathtaking global dominance, seeming invincibility, and stunning success in redistributing the world's resources ever upward. And during that same decade, the liberal reform branches of the U.S.-based social movements of the 1960s and 1970s crept ever rightward, increasingly abandoning the broad social, cultural, economic, and political critiques and transformative visions that once fed them. Lobbying, litigating, and fundraising replaced mass mobilization and public dissent as primary modes of activism for equality, even as the operative definition of "equality" narrowed dramatically enough, in some liberal reformist circles, to make peace with neoliberalism.

For instance: The reproductive freedom and women's health movement that thrived during the 1960s and 1970s generated a broad critique of the cultural and material forces constraining women's reproductive and sexual lives. An extensive network of local organizations and mobilizations, focused on sterilization abuse as well as abortion rights, on broad-based women's health activism as well as on legal strategies, on sexual as well as reproductive freedom, affiliated to form the Reproductive Rights National Network. During the 1980s and 1990s, this field of social activism, and the critique of the medical establishment and drug industry's profit-making ploys as well as their patriarchal hierarchies and racist agendas, largely receded from public view (and at the same time, the medical industry morphed into new corporate forms, including Health Maintenance Organizations, that diffused activist challenges). Broad-based feminist health activism persisted, but narrow, single-issue lobbying, litigation, and fundraising organizations such as the National Abortion Rights Action League (NARAL) emerged to focus action and energy on the defense of *Roe v. Wade*. NARAL, like HRC (see chapter 3), endorses politicians on the sole basis of support for *Roe v. Wade*, regardless of the rest of the politician's record.[1]

This general trend was not the whole story, however. The environmental movement, for example, developed into a narrow environmental "preservation" establishment on the one hand, yet generated a rapidly proliferating, politically vital environmental justice movement on the other.[2] And, at the same time that the goals of feminist, antiracist, democratically accessible reproductive and sexual freedom narrowed to "private" abortion rights, the movement to prevent and treat HIV infection and AIDS grew. AIDS activism exhibited all the conflicts and contradictions of liberal vs. radical strategies, legalistic political reform vs. cultural transformation, local vs. national and global agendas. Its organizations and institutions were (and are) marked by racism, sexism, and North American–centered arrogance. But AIDS activism became and remains an expansive social movement within which radical critiques and broad visions of democracy and equality, passed on in part from earlier local, national, and global women's health activism, have flourished around the world.[3]

These forms of progressive thinking and activism survived, and some even thrived during the 1980s and 1990s, mostly below the radar of national politics and media. By the end of the 1990s, as neoliberalism began to falter—an effect of worldwide opposition to its policies as well as to its evident failures—new opportunities and dangers for progressive-left organizing began to appear on the political horizon of the new millennium. Encouraged by increasing mass opposition to neoliberal policies around the world, in Latin America especially, U.S.-based activists mobilized a stunning display of public fury directed at global financial elites meeting in Seattle, Washington, during fall 1999. This mobilization was not so much the birth of a new social movement— as many surprised pundits opined—but rather the coming together and public coming-out of widely divergent and dispersed progressive forces. The decentralized nature of this mass mobilization, though often lamented as a sign of disorganization, signaled an opportunity—an opening for the emergence of a radically democratic left, with a global vision and global connections, that might once again offer a field for the cross-fertilization of progressive thought and action, and a context for overcoming, rather than reproducing, the fragmentation and disconnections of the previous two decades.[4]

As global opposition worked to expose the ruses of neoliberalism during the late 1990s, and to reveal the naked power relations and cultural projects underpinning its ostensibly neutral, managerial principles, the political landscape suddenly and dramatically shifted on September 11, 2001. Even as the world grieved for the thousands of lives lost in the rubble of downtown New York City, speculation and critical analysis about underlying causes of Arab resentment of the U.S. began circulating widely. These analyses linked with critical analyses of corporate power, international financial institutions, and U.S. dominance in many parts of the world.[5]

As this conversation expanded in the months following 9/11, the facade of benevolence and of global good works for the benefit ultimately of all, was blasted away from U.S.-based corporate aspirations for peaceful "globalization." The question "Why do they hate us?" made the rounds of baffled pundits as the extent of resentment against the institutions of global financial coercion, represented by the World Trade Towers, and against the political power and military force underpinning their dominance, represented by the Pentagon and the White House, became apparent. As government PR spin and corporate media conglomerates focused on the threat of terrorism from Muslim fundamentalists, government surveillance escalated, and a crackdown on dissent worked to discredit the other analyses of the meanings of 9/11 as "unpatriotic."[6]

Just as it seemed that the Bush administration might largely succeed in manufacturing consent for so-called antiterror measures curtailing the freedom to speak, write, travel, and organize, two additional fronts in the battle against U.S. corporate and state power opened up. The stock market bubble of the 1990s burst, and corporate scandals exposed mind-boggling greed, widespread fraud, and extensive corruption at the top of powerful corporations, including those with close ties to the White House. Then just as public disaffection with broken corporate promises and vast persistent economic injustices grew at a threatening pace, Bush and company began to promote war fever against Iraq. Resistance to that agenda in Europe exposed the widespread "anti-Americanism" there, and it suddenly became clearer that "Why do they hate us?" was a question to be asked about many Europeans and other populations in other parts of the world in addition to Muslim religious fanatics.

The realities of economic disaster and the collapse of social supports under neoliberal policies around the globe, and the threat and experience of violence, so undeniable now, make the world an increasingly dangerous and tragic place. But they also expose neoliberalism as a ruse of neo-imperialism, founded in force and coercion, rather than the program for world peace, prosperity, and democracy through "free" markets" and "free" trade that its avatars promote. Or rather, they *might* expose neoliberal coercion and inequality *if* progressive-left forces around the world can seize the opportunity, in the face of danger and tragedy, to connect, circulate ideas and information, expand the bases of opposition to neoliberalism, and nurture alternative visions.

To seize the opportunities of the twenty-first century, progressive social movements need deeper and broader analyses of the workings of neoliberalism. Because neoliberalism is not a unitary "system," but a complex, contradictory cultural and political project created within specific institutions, with an agenda for reshaping the everyday life of contemporary global capitalism, analyses of its recent history and hopefully future demise must be diverse, contingent, flexibly attuned to historical change, and open to constant debate and revision. Neoliberal politics must be understood *in relation to* coexisting, conflicting, shifting relations of power along multiple lines of difference and hierarchy. Developing analyses of neoliberalism must ask how the many local alliances, cultural projects, nationalist agendas, and economic policies work together, unevenly and often unpredictably, rife with conflict and contradiction, to redistribute the world's resources up-ward—money, security, healthcare, and mobility; knowledge and ac-cess to communication technologies; leisure, recreation, and pleasure; freedom—to procreate or not, to be sexually expressive or not, to work or not; political power—participatory access to democratic public life, and more . . . in short, resources of all kinds.

One of the primary blocks to this kind of analysis, and to the growth of social movements to redistribute resources downward in the wake of neoliberalism's hoped for demise, is the split within the pro-gressive-left between so-called identity and cultural politics on the one side, and the mutating contemporary forms of left universalism, economism, and populism on the other. Within the U.S., the specific dynamic of identity-based political formations drifting rightward into neoliberalism's embrace, while being denigrated and dismissed on the progressive-left with increasing ferocity, is a self-propelling, self-defeating, utterly antiproductive spiral of political schism. The more that identity and cultural politics are represented as the irresponsible, trivial, divisive "other" of serious left analysis and organizing, the more constituencies seeking equality may be alienated from the left and abandoned to claim redress through liberal reform alone. This alien-ation of potential constituencies drains the left of creativity and vital-ity as well as reducing its body counts. And, without the analytic and organizing energy found within the identity-based political forma-tions, the progressive-left has no hope of effectively grasping the forces it seeks to arrest and reverse—those promoting antidemocratic in-equality on multiple fronts.

This problem of dismissal and schism appears in many forms—in local, national, and global activism, and in political analysis and schol-arship. For example: During the late 1990s, the Working Family Party formed in New York state to offer a progressive alternative to the two major political parties. Drawing on the strong populist tradition in U.S. politics, the WFP sought to appeal to the economic interests of work-ing New Yorkers who were losing ground to the wealthy throughout the decade. In a misguided effort to be inclusive, WFP downplayed its sup-

port of feminist goals including reproductive freedom, muted its attention to racial politics, and avoided public mention of support for lesbian, gay, bisexual and transgender New Yorkers. If the WFP thereby
managed to maintain the support of some homophobic white racist
patriarchs, it also lost the attention and potential energy of large constituencies who did not believe they could afford to leave the Democratic Party, and the tepid support it offered, for the back-seat-only
accommodations on the WFP bus.[7]

This split was played out on a national scale during the 2000 presidential campaign, as the Green Party candidacy of consumer advocate
and corporate critic Ralph Nader temporarily threatened the Gore
campaign's lock on liberal and progressive votes. As Nader's support
grew, the Gore campaign recruited representatives from identity-based
politics—including Gloria Steinem, Jesse Jackson, and Barney Frank—
to stump for the Democrats and attack Nader and the Green Party's
record on feminist, antiracist and lesbian and gay issues. Despite Gore's
neoliberal agenda, and the superficiality and unreliability of Democratic Party support for the elimination of identity-based exclusions
in public life, this strategy was often effective. Though the Nader campaign's stated support for equality and inclusion along lines of race,
gender and sexuality was generally stronger than the Gore campaign's,
no analysis of these social hierarchies and their relation to the political
economy was offered. Therefore, the specific "identity" issues were
defined as matters of simple "discrimination," and treated as decidedly
secondary, even dispensable, by the candidate.

In a widely publicized gaffe during an appearance on ABC's *This
Week*, Nader commented that, in the unlikely event that *Roe v. Wade*
was overturned by the Supreme Court, all would not be lost, as juris-
diction and the political battle would revert to the states. This effort
to minimize the possibly major differences between a Bush presidency
vs. a Gore administration (and thus to minimize the "cost" of a Green
Party vote) also implied that the loss of *Roe v. Wade* would not be a
national disaster. Nader therefore seemed to confirm the charges of indifference to women's issues emanating from the Gore campaign. And

when he was quoted as referring to lesbian and gay issues as "gonadal politics," this trivialization and dismissal was also widely noted (though not solidly confirmed).[8]

Beyond the attack politics of election campaigns, this split between the Gore and Nader camps had a wider resonance—reflecting and reproducing the split between so-called identity politics and economic justice campaigns. The fundamental sticking point was expressed by Nader in his memoir, *Crashing the Party: Taking on the Corporate Government in an Age of Surrender*:

> Being a progressive presidential candidate meant far more than being an identity politics candidate. It meant going to the roots of the power abuses of our political economy. If I made one mistake in addressing the identity politics adherents, it was not putting forth a detailed record of my past writings and involvement against racial and gender discrimination going back to the midfifties.[9]

It is nonetheless apparent that Nader made more than one mistake. In referring to "progressive" politics as "more than" identity politics, arguing that the former goes to the "roots" of the power abuses of the political economy and the other doesn't, Nader produced a schism and a hierarchy of seriousness and importance in his own rhetoric. Nader spoke as if the "political economy" might be abstracted from racial, gendered, and sexual hierarchies, rather than understood as operating through them. His campaign's treatment of "identity" issues as "less than" was not merely describing the political landscape, in which identity politics formations varied widely in the extent of their engagements with the political economy's abuses. The campaign rhetoric was also producing the very split being lamented—by provoking the flight of wavering but wary constituencies into the neoliberal Democratic ranks.

Outside the arena of U.S. electoral politics, in the global arena of mobilizations against neoliberal policies, many activists, writers, and organizers have also tended to denigrate, trivialize, or sideline "identity" issues. The predominant whiteness of the Seattle demonstrations, for instance, raised questions about the social locations and presumptions of the political base and strategies of the U.S. organizers.[10] Naomi Klein's best-selling, sharp, and inspirational critique of corporate dominance, *No Logo*, offers one clear view into the nature and operations of such unwitting exclusions on the left. Klein characterizes "identity politics" as the superficial politics of representation, easily accommodated by corporate media as "diversity" or niche marketing. But Klein refers only to the campus activism of her younger years, significantly during the 1980s, as a basis for this characterization—a profound reduction, in both the historical range and the social bases for identity politics. Using this shrunken remnant, Klein constructs an "other" for serious, adult progressive politics, even as she expresses support for the general goals of the politics she thus consigns to the margins, or to the past. When she writes that,

> Dinesh D'Souza and his ilk couldn't resist calling the PC'ers "neo-Marxists"—but, in fact, nothing could have been further from the truth. The prospect of having to change a few pronouns and getting a handful of women and minorities on the board and on television posed no real threat to the guiding profit-making principles of Wall Street.... [11]

Klein reduces the efforts of socialist feminists and women-of-color organizers, gay leftists and ACT-UP activists, reproductive freedom fighters and black radicals by ... equating them with the efforts of her friends in college to get "women and minorities" on the board of trustees?

The point of such reductive accounts of identity politics—rooted almost exclusively in examples from the most narrow and balkanized forms of post-1980s equality activism among privileged youth—is to represent the current progressive activism of the writer as serious, mature and truly radical by contrast. Yet she also notes that her own recent anticorporate activism has also been quickly absorbed into corporate advertising and marketing campaigns—the contrast she creates does not hold up even under her own unselfconscious scrutiny. The stark either/or framing, of identity politics vs. progressive activism, is both distorted and counterproductive.

Another huge-selling indictment of neoliberal market utopianism, Thomas Frank's *One Market Under God: Extreme Capitalism, Market Populism, and the End of Economic Democracy* indicts academic "cultural studies" on grounds similar to those Klein finds for dismissing identity politics—the market populists of the corporate culture industries have resonated to the celebrations of popular culture, and to the resistant agency of audiences described by cultural studies scholars, and have found ways to make profitable use of similar notions. This is a very slippery hat trick, as it ascribes all importance to the corporate arena. The logic is: If corporations can make profitable use of an idea, it is a bad idea. Yet Anchor Books, a division of Random House, itself a division of the international media conglomerate Bertelsmann AG (not exactly a public interest organization), is making very profitable use of Frank's ideas.[12]

In the case of "cultural studies," now almost as automatically trivializing a designation as "identity politics" in some quarters on the left, the meticulous attention to political economy, the engagement with political organizing outside the university and the consistently anticorporate agenda of the field is ignored by Frank (and many other critics) in one long self-congratulatory smirk. Such dismissals do not constitute engaged political dialogue, but serve the function of contemptuously exiling entire contingents of progressive intellectual activists. It is hard to conceive of this as a productive move for "serious" political organizing.

The division of identity vs. progressive/class politics is not confined to activists and journalists, but also characterizes much recent left political history, theory, and scholarship as well. One of the most widely cited critiques of so-called identity politics from the left, media studies scholar and former New Left activist Todd Gitlin's 1995 polemic *The Twilight of Common Dreams*, offers a decline-and-fall-of-the-left story

with a clear chronology and a villain—a monstrous amalgam of impo-
tent and misdirected rage, reactionary separatism and trivializing politics ... "identity politics"! In about 1975, Gitlin argues, the New Left of
universalist hope gave way to the New Left of separatist rage, and the
possibility of a broadly engaging, effective left was lost. He acknowl-
edges that New Left "universalism" was limited, and that many com-
plaints from identity-based formations were justified, even beneficial.
But when he looks for the causes of the decline of progressive effectiveness in national political life, he assigns it not to political economic
changes or to conservative or neoliberal attacks, or to a series of flaws,
failures, lost opportunities, and weaknesses across the left political
spectrum, but to the destructive impact of identity politics.[13]

It is relatively easy to assemble a list of the Stupid Political Tricks of
any social movement or political grouping, and Gitlin's effort to assemble such a list to indict "identity politics" reflects and repeats the
previous efforts of conservative moralists and culture warriors. One
might quickly assemble a similarly impressive list for the "universalist"
New Left, but why bother? Gitlin's list is interesting not for its revela-
tion of obnoxious stupidities, but for his overall definition of "identity
politics" and his assessment of its wrong turns.

Like Andrew Sullivan, Gitlin constructs a monstrous political
"other" that turns out to be rather hard to pin down. The "they" that
he describes keeps shifting, referring to very different political group-
ings often at odds with each other; he then assigns flaws he finds in
one group to all the others, often completely erroneously. He lumps together Foucauldian academics with cultural feminists, who are not dis-
tinguished from "difference" feminists who might be poststructuralists
—but we are not sure! Cultural studies and cultural politics are merged
into political tribalism, or reverence for "tradition" ... ? When he writes
that "they" declared the death of humanism, while resorting to legalistic regulation to address social problems—launching antipornography
campaigns and supporting speech codes—well, he's got some apples
and oranges in his basket of rocks. The "they" who have ruined the left
turn out to be *all* political formations with which he disagrees, no mat-

ter how politically distant from each other. And "identity politics" turns out to be a floating signifier, interchangeable with "cultural politics" or posthumanist theory, applicable to any and all progressive-left or liberal reformist critiques of *either* universalism or humanism.

From a different quarter but in a similar vein, philosophical pragmatist Richard Rorty's 1997 *Achieving Our Country* attributes the decline and fall of the left to the "Cultural Left," which is a fallen form of the "Reformist Left" and the "New Left." Though Rorty blames Marxists for a lot of wrong-headedness as well, he assigns the primary responsibility for a retreat from "real" politics to a party of academics, especially Foucauldians, who have invested in the wrong term in a series of binaries: political economy vs. philosophy (useless for politics), money vs. stigma (less important), agency vs. spectatorship (obviously bad), critiques of selfishness vs. critiques of sadism (again, not as important). Though Rorty argues for bridging and connecting these terms in most cases (though he has very little good to say about philosophy), he separates them as alternative emphases and arranges them in a hierarchy, then opposes the Reformist Left as the party of the high terms and the Cultural Left as the party of the low.

When Rorty comes out in this book confessing, "I was a teenage Cold War liberal," the reader begins to understand the reference points for his political alignments. But like Gitlin, his standpoint is more narcissistic than sociological, ethnographic, or historical. He is training his critical eye on the academics around him, daily, and finding fault with the theoretical moves and political locations of a motley crew, from cultural studies professors, to women's or ethnic studies programs, to Foucauldian philosophers or Lacanian film critics. What they have in common is their proximity to Rorty and their progressive-left commitments, as well as some difference from his political views.[14]

But where is the rest of the progressive-left? Or even, to use his term, what might be called a Cultural Left? Oh...for instance, hip-hop groups, women's music festival organizers, gay and lesbian antiviolence projects, punk anarchists, Latino writers, Asian-American filmmakers, Native American environmentalists, and on and on. If he were serious about locating and analyzing such a formation, he would immediately find himself overwhelmed by the range of liberal to left politics, often unclassifiable in such terms, and the multiple modes of engagement with the interlocking realms of the state, the political economy (of which, last I heard, the culture industries constitute a part, and not some "other" cultural space separable from wealth production and resource distribution), civil society, and the family form. For instance, how might Rorty classify Alisa Solomon's activist journalism (cited in chapter 2, and in reference to the Working Families Party, above)? Solomon writes about money *and* stigma, selfishness *and* sadism, as they are inseparably intertwined in the neoliberal culture wars. Her political/cultural writing—about the irreducible interrelations among the inadequate and mystifying liberal categories of the state, the economy, civil and intimate life—is simply unclassifiable in the Rortian universe.

In the end, writers including Gitlin and Rorty can be understood as advocating that one progressive-left formation, the one that they felt allegiance to in their youth (the New Left for Gitlin, the Reformist Left for Rorty), be updated and expanded in familiar form as the *whole* left. Other progressive- left formations—a vast range from liberal reformist civil rights lobbies to poststructuralist philosophers, from ethnic studies programs to lesbian separatists—are being *admonished* to fall in line, to get real, to take instruction, and well ... to grow up. The overwhelming force of the charges against identity and cultural politics is an imputation of infantilism, vs. the maturity of the writer's stance. Can we look through the spray of words and see "childish" written over the indistinguishable politics of people of color, women, queers, and ... their academic representatives and advocates, however otherwise dissimilar their political/scholarly profiles?

As reductive and dismissive as Gitlin and Rorty can be, they are respectful by comparison to some writers sharing their general points. For instance, Michael Tomasky, in his 1997 book *Left for Dead*, sinks to an insulting low when he asks,

Who profits when left and right are locked in cultural battle over epidermis and genitalia? For the people who own the country, this battle is a pure godsend....[15]

But critiques of "identity politics" have come from within as well as from outside the political formations generally designated by this term. Such internal critiques have often been friendly, jocular, ironic, or self-critical. But they have also been enlisted to make distinctions of value, not completely unlike those made by Gitlin and Rorty.

Wendy Brown's powerful 1995 critique of liberalism, *States of Injury*, exhibits a kind of split personality with regard to contemporary identity politics. On the one hand, Brown calls for historically specific accounts and multiple frames of reference for thinking through the impact and considering the future of such political formations. On the other hand, Brown leaps to a characterization/critique of identity-based movements as not only eschewing class politics, but as naturalizing capitalism. The problem with this move is *not* that Brown is wrong; identity-based politics *have* operated, rhetorically and practically, in just the way she describes. The problem is that she overgeneralizes, wipes out the very historical specificity she elsewhere calls for, and insists in the end on abstracting some overall or general effect of "identity politics" from its most conservative/neoliberal instantiations. How is this helpful? Wouldn't keeping the most radically transformative and creative moments at the forefront of political analysis be more generative?

Then there is another problem with Brown's analysis. Like Gitlin or Rorty, she produces an opposition that is clearly hierarchical, positions herself unwaveringly on the high end, and adopts a one-sided pedagogical mode laced with a tone of admonishment, and even sometimes contempt, in addressing the low end. In *States of Injury* she describes the political battle over an antidiscrimination ordinance in Berkeley, California, as an example of the typical mistakes and excesses of identity politics—the reification of attributes for protection from discrimination into a long list, including sexual orientation, race, gender, disability, etc. This example is mobilized within her argument for the primary purpose of lampooning the "misguided" activists, whose silliness and narrowness underwrite her own serious breadth by contrast. Might her reading of the campaign's rhetoric and tactics be flattening, stripping it of all nuance and struggle to exceed available "identity" categories, reducing the aspirations of the range of participants to the narrowest possible liberal frame permitted within U.S. legislative discourse? Might another kind of political writer (someone like the engaged activist-critic Cindy Patton perhaps) find in this battle a wider range of political aspirations and a field of contention with moments of transformative, even anticapitalist and antiliberal creativity?[16]

The impulse to caricature identity or cultural politics as political "other" underwrites the critic's authority more than it usefully describes the political landscape. This impulse leads Brown to misdescribe as well as overgeneralize—not only about identity politics, but about the overall history of liberal to left politics in the United States. In her 2002 article "Moralism as Antipolitics" she argues that,

> Neither leftists nor liberals are free of the idea of progress in history. Neither can conceive of freedom or equality without rights, sovereignty, and the state, and hence without the figures of a sovereign subject and a neutral state.[17]

Um, excuse me? U.S. history is thickly populated with leftists who conceived of equality and freedom in critical relation to a very nonneutral state, and even U.S. social democratic liberals have exhibited far more savvy strategy than deep belief in the efficacy of "rights" than Brown will allow. But this kind of reductive condensation enables the pedagogical mode. Brown ultimately wants to offer "advice" to the progressive-left and its errant identity politics wings—to hue to a language of politic "wanting" rather than "being." But the language of "wanting" or political desire, and the critique of fixed ontologies of "being," have been present *within* left, radical, identity and cultural politics all along—as Robin Kelley's *Freedom Dreams: The Black Radical Imagination* has recently impressively documented.[18]

This pedagogical mode infuses much leftist and feminist academic writing about political activism. Mary Poovey's analysis of reproductive rights and abortion politics in the U.S. is in many ways typical. Poovey analyses the limits of liberal "privacy" and "rights" discourse in the battle for access to safe and legal abortion, and in pedagogical mode advises that activists turn instead to a language emphasizing women's reproductive health. Poovey's critique is incisive and persuasive. The problem is that Poovey seems completely unaware of the existence of the Reproductive Rights National Network and the extensive deployment of just such an emphasis on women's health, together with a critique of medical capitalism as well as "privacy" and rights" language, by those affiliated groups and activists. She seems unable to imagine, as well, that many of the activists and lawyers who argued the abortion cases in liberal language in U.S. courtrooms were familiar with and sympathetic to critiques like Poovey's, but made tactical decisions about how to "win," given the high costs of illegal abortion. A dialogue about the costs of this kind of tactical decision might have offered more valuable insight than a pedagogically motivated rehearsal of the left/feminist critique of "privacy" and "rights."[19]

This common pedagogical mode seems counterproductive for political engagement, and is too often based on incomplete knowledge of the history of the social movements being "taught." Rather than admonish and advise, it would make more political sense to *locate, engage,* and *expand* productive political moments for future elaboration.

Some writers on the socialist and feminist left make the distinction between identity or cultural politics and economic justice campaigns *without* producing a hierarchy or adopting a condescending pedagogical voice. Nancy Fraser's widely influential version of a distinction between the politics of *recognition* and the politics of *redistribution*, first articulated in *Justice Interruptus* (1997), very carefully notes that these are *analytical* distinctions, and not a real world separation between intertwined political histories. Fraser never explicitly produces a hierarchy or adopts a pedagogical mode, and she further complicates the binary she describes with another crosscutting distinction between *affirmative* and *transformative* remedies. The politics of recognition, which is addressed to injurious status differences rather than to the operations of the economy, might affirm identity in the context of liberal reform, or advocate radical transformation of cultural categories. The politics of redistribution might argue in the affirmative mode for limited equalizing alterations in capitalism and the state, or envision a socialist transformation of the institutions of political economy.

Fraser's goals—to formulate a nonidentitarian politics of recognition that doesn't displace redistribution, or slide into essentialist tribalism—are directed toward overcoming the identity politics/left economism split by elaborating the most progressive tendencies on each side. Yet her reiteration of the distinction, in a predominantly static rather than dynamic relation to each other and to the institutions of political economy, tends to entrench the split she describes in ways that implicitly recreate the hierarchy she eschews.[20]

These problems in her argument are the most apparent in her exchange with Judith Butler in *Social Text* (1997). Butler argues that Fraser's spectrum from redistribution (illustrated by class politics) to recognition (illustrated by "merely cultural" lesbian, gay, and queer politics) effectively cordons off the political economic critique embedded in political critiques labeled as cultural, and takes the economist left off the hook of accounting for the work of sexuality, specifically (though not only), in the distribution of material resources. Butler draws on 1970s socialist feminism, and especially on the work of Gayle Rubin, to recover the argument that sexual regulation is a core component in historically changing modes of economic distribution.

As Butler points out, Fraser's spectrum is loaded with a distortion that truncates the force and range of queer politics. Fraser argues that class politics focus primarily on distribution, only very secondarily on recognition. She then analyzes the politics of gender and race as hybrid forms, combining aspects of distribution and recognition. But she places queer politics on the recognition end of the spectrum, credited with only a very secondary emphasis on distribution. But if class politics are *also* fundamentally about recognition—of laborers and the unemployed as full members and sharers in collective life, and queer politics critique the family and its supportive relation to forms of hierarchy and exploitative labor, then all kinds of politics are hybrid forms. The spectrum itself, designed to in some sense quantify the "levels" of recognition and distribution emphasized in differing political formations, makes an invidious distinction masquerading as a benign one. To place queer politics under the label of a purely "cultural" politics of recognition, denies that queer analysis addresses political economy, material life, and the history of modes of production and reproduction of social life, at the center of analysis. This kind of reduction then produces an implicit hierarchy where no explicit one exists, by stripping "cultural" critique or identity politics of their capacity to engage and transform political economy. The most conservative/neoliberal forms of "identity politics"—forms that in fact do not offer any political economic critique—are substituted for the radical critiques informing feminist queer, antiracist political creativity.[21]

Unfortunately, Fraser's response to Butler in the *Social Text* exchange misses the fundamental point of her critique. Butler's effort to demonstrate that the distinction between political economy and culture is unstable and politically unproductive is met with Fraser's charge that this is a *deconstructive* argument, rather than a more illuminating *historical* one. Fraser argues that capitalism creates a distinction between status and class, and that the divisions reflected in her analysis follow from the development of this real historical distinction. But Fraser misses the fundamentally historical dimension of Butler's critique. Butler is not "merely deconstructing" the economy/culture distinction, she is demonstrating that the distinction is a kind of *ruse* of capitalist liberal discourse—a ruse that obscures the intricate imbrications of relations of race, gender, sexuality, and class in the institutions of capitalist modernity. As a historical matter, status and class are not separated by capitalism, which operates through status categories at every stage of its historical development. Status and class are rhetorically disarticulated (in the U.S. this occurs during the early decades of the nineteenth century) in order to remove capitalism from the demands of even a limited, purely formal democracy of white men (see chapter 1). This ruse of formal distinction, rather than real separation, is one that Fraser has fallen into and replicated, rather than exposed and transformed.

Butler is the better historian in this exchange with Fraser, though her argument is suggested rather than developed. The future elaboration of Butler's analysis, itself based on a recovery of the arguments of socialist feminism, would need to offer an account that addresses the centrality of racial differentiation, together with gender and sexuality, in the history of liberal capitalism in the West. An historical/political analysis that resists the dominant distinctions of capitalist liberalism—those between class and political economy versus status or "identity" and culture (marked as they are by the master rhetoric of public vs. private)—would do more to generate progressive political engagements across current divides than any rehearsal of a static recognition/redistribution distinction ever could.

Paul Gilroy's *Against Race* offers something like this kind of analysis. His critique of liberal humanism and its contemporary other, racial and ethnic or identity absolutism, is embedded in a critique of globalizing commercial capitalism and its racialized imaginaries. His calls for a radical planetary humanism, for cosmopolitanism and democracy, and for a notion of identity as a kind of process (he refers to diasporic identity as a model for this) work to fundamentally reframe the terms of Western humanism. Gilroy proposes a progressive politics that does not erase racial difference, and its central historical role as a term of brutal hierarchy as well as of resistance to hierarchy, but that takes racial identities as multiple, changing, and crosscut by other social and cultural identity categories.[22]

Gilroy's text does adopt a pedagogical tone, however. The primary critical target for his critique of racial absolutism is the Nation of Islam

and Louis Farrakhan, though he adds examples from black popular culture, and from writing by academics and public intellectuals. Such
examples do not really add up to the pervasive popularity and fashion-
ableness of identity absolutes—he ends up reducing a complex field of
racial politics to a somewhat flattened landscape of good/diasporic and
bad/absolutist identities. When he turns from examples to generaliza-
tions, one is often left with the question Robin Kelley posed to Michael
Tomasky's account of identity politics: *Who is he talking about?* His
readings can be reductively hostile—for example, the Elizabeth Alexander essay that Gilroy critiques for its biologism might be interpreted
quite differently. Alexander's black body might be read as a metaphoric
social body, rather than as a scientific body (she *is* a poet, among other
things). And his accounts of political life can be focused somewhat
askew. Even his central bad example, Farrakhan's version of Black Nationalism, becomes a much more complex and contradiction-ridden
field if one looks at the social movement rather than primarily at the
leader (as, for instance, in the work of Wahneema Lubiano).[23]

Robin D. G. Kelley proposes, and continually enacts, ways of mobilizing currently fractured progressive social movements by building on
dynamic, interactive differences—rather than bracketing or enshrining
them. In *Yo Mama's Disfunktional!* Kelley proposes generating unity
through a set of affliations constructed by supporting and participating
in other people's struggles for social justice. He argues that though identity politics sometimes fetters multiracial/multicultural left politics, it
has also often enriched the conception of class rather than displaced it.
Kelley insists that it isn't possible to organize along class lines if the way
class is actually lived, through race, gender, and sexuality among other
modes, is marginalized or ignored. In *Freedom Dreams* Kelley reads a
document that might be offered as an example of fractious identity-
mongering, the 1970s black feminist manifesto *The Combahee River
Statement,* and names it one of the most important documents of the
black radical movement in the twentieth century. Kelley finds in this
document, the product of a collective social movement, a kind of uni-

versalism with more to offer the left than the totalizing universalisms, majoritarianism and hegemonic nationalism of what he calls the Neo-Enlightenment Left (Gitlin, Rorty, Tomasky and others).[24]

Eric Lott, in his critical examination of left/liberal universalism, offered by a cohort of social democrats he calls the "boomer liberals," also argues that identity political movements are misdescribed by critics of so-called cultural politics. Critics focus on the identities, and overlook politics—which is a way not to take any of it seriously. Lott calls for a politics of *participatory discrepancy:*

> This kind of situation, I think, is what one gets "after" identity politics: a politics of *participatory discrepancy* that comes about as a congeries of new social movements jostle, collide, and sometimes collude in broad transmovement desires.[25]

This proposal, similar to Kelley's concept of affiliation, is not in the least pedagogical—it constitutes an expansion of the hopeful moments of actually existing politics.

This critically engaged but generous and generative spirit animates the conversation between writer/activist Amber Hollibaugh and academic/activist Nikhil Pal Singh published in the anthology *Out at Work: Building a Gay-Labor Alliance.* Hollibaugh and Singh examine the new labor politics, looking for signs of political convergence and synergy among labor organizers and new social movement veterans. They critique left universalists for wanting to *reprivatize* whole landscapes of social life, the lived modalities of race, gender, and sexuality, in ways that impoverish labor organizing, as well as left politics generally. Hollibaugh points to the history of AIDS politics, noting that activists *could not* bracket the impact of race, class, gender, sexuality, religion, or nationality and still hope to be effective. Identity categories morphed, from *gay men* to *men who have sex with men,* and expanded, to include the vast populations of the world's working and workless poor who have become the pandemic's victims. Critiques of political economy, in which the medical establishment and drug trade are embedded, and which produces the brutal inequalities that feed the disease, were necessarily aligned with cultural and identity-based politics, in some quarters if not in all.[26]

Hollibaugh's account of AIDS politics offers an incisive critique of any economy/culture split, and makes the recognition/redistribution binary appear as a false dualism. Other active social movements provide such critiques as well: the movement for abolition of the prison industrial complex, the environmental justice campaign, and the mobilizations in opposition to welfare "reform." Some activist institutions also resist these splits and binaries, including for example the Audre Lorde Project in New York City, which organizes queers of color (lesbian, gay, bisexual, transgendered and two-spirit New Yorkers, from all over the globe) to address issues from immigration and HIV prevention, to violence and employment issues. These fields of analysis and activity provide creative links among identity-based politics, social democratic reform, and utopian, flexible left unities.

Radical social movements and activist institutions often reach beyond the liberal categories of collective life—the state, the economy, civil society, and the family—to transcend and overcome their mystifications and mutually constituting inequalities. Calls for expansive democratic publicness, *combined* with arguments for forms of individual and group autonomy, attempt to redefine *equality, freedom, justice,* and *democracy* in ways that exceed their limited (neo)liberal meanings. They gesture away from *privatization* as an alibi for stark inequalities, and away from *personal responsibility* as an abdication of public, collective caretaking. Such efforts are all too frequently misheard by analysts and critics who do not listen for the moments of rupture in the language of transformative politics, but who hear reductively, seeking only familiar repetitions. But careful listening, in the modes of Robin Kelley, Eric Lott, Wahneema Lubiano, Cindy Patton, Amber Hollibaugh, or Nikhil Singh, reveals political desires beyond the economy/culture split, and its disciplining authority.

Now, at this moment of danger and opportunity, the progressive-left is mobilizing against neoliberalism and possible new or continuing wars. These mobilizations might become sites for factional struggles over the disciplining of the troops, in the name of unity at a time of crisis and necessity. But such efforts will fail; the troops will not be disciplined, and the disciplinarians will be left to their bitterness. Or, we might find ways of thinking, speaking, writing, and acting that are engaged and curious about "other people's" struggles for social justice, that are respectfully affiliative and dialogic rather than pedagogical, that look for the hopeful spots to expand upon, and that revel in the pleasure of political life. For it is pleasure *and* collective caretaking, love *and* the egalitarian circulation of money—allied to clear and hard-headed political analysis offered generously—that will create the space for a progressive politics that might both imagine and create ... something worth living for.

Notes

Introduction

1. For an illuminating account of the limited "social warrant" of the 1930s, based on higher wages for white male workers and on an expanded "warfare" as well as welfare state, see George Lipsitz, *American Studies in a Moment of Danger* (Minneapolis: University of Minnesota Press, 2001). In chapter 4, Lipsitz outlines the attacks on both the Age of the CIO (1930s) and the Age of the Civil Rights movement (1960s) during the 1970s and 1980s—attacks fomented by a powerful coalition of multinational corporations, small property holders, independent entrepreneurs, and religious fundamentalists.

2. My discussion of the history of Liberalism, here and in chapter 1, is necessarily highly truncated. The literature on this topic is vast. For good introductions, see Karl Polanyi, *The Great Transformation* (Boston: Beacon Press, 1944) and Wendy Brown, "Liberalism's Family Values" in her *States of Injury* (Princeton, N.J.: Princeton University Press, 1995), pp. 135–165.

3. For varying but nonetheless overlapping outlines of the features and agenda of neoliberalism, see Jean and John L. Comaroff, editors, "Millennial Capitalism and the Culture of Neoliberalism," a special issue of *Public Culture*, 12, no. 2 (Spring 2000); Noam Chomsky, *Profit Over People: Neoliberalism and Global Order* (New York: Seven Stories Press, 1999); and David Boaz, editor, *Toward Liberty: The Idea That Is Changing the World* (Washington, D.C.: The Cato Institute, 2002).

4. As I will argue more extensively in chapter 1, *identity politics* in the broadest sense arises from the exclusions of the U.S. nation-state beginning in the early nineteenth century. But *identity politics* in the narrowest sense defined here first appeared in the 1980s.

5. See any of a long list of publications by Cindy Patton, including *Inventing AIDS* (New York: Routledge, 1990), *Last Served? Gendering the HIV Pandemic* (New York: Taylor and Francis, 1994), and *Globalizing AIDS* (Minneapolis: University of Minnesota Press, 2002).

Chapter 1, Downsizing Democracy

1. Kevin Phillips, *Wealth and Democracy: A Political History of the American Rich* (New York: Broadway Books, 2002), pp. xii, 412.

2. *New York Times*, "The Week in Review," 30 June 2002, p. 1; Joseph E. Stiglitz, *Globalization and Its Discontents* (New York and London: W. W. Norton, 2002); and Phillips, *Wealth and Democracy*.

3. The literature on the history of capitalism and Liberalism is vast. For good introductions see Karl Polanyi, *The Great Transformation* (Boston: Beacon Press, 1944)
   and Wendy Brown, "Liberalism's Family Values" in *States of Injury* (Princeton, N.J.:
   Princeton University Press, 1995), pp. 135–165.

4. For an interesting account of this process, see Kathleen McHugh, *American Domesticity* (New York: Oxford University Press, 1999).

5. See Timothy Mitchell, "Society, Economy, and the State Effect," in George Stein-
   metz, editor, *State/Culture: State-Formation after the Cultural Turn* (Ithaca and Lon-
   don: Cornell University Press, 1999), pp. 76–97; David Lloyd and Paul Thomas,
   Culture and the State (New York and London: Routledge, 1998); Michael A. Peters,
   Poststructuralism, Marxism and Neoliberalism: Between Theory and Politics (New
   York and Oxford: Rowman, Littlefield Publishers, Inc., 2001).

6. There were some occasions of connection and overlap in organizations such as
   the Knights of Labor, for instance, or through the work of activists such as Emma
   Goldman.

7. For an analysis of neoliberalism's history and impact, see the special issue of *Public
   Culture*, "Millennial Capitalism and the Culture of Neoliberalism," 12, no. 2 (spring
   2000), especially the introductory essay by the volume editors, Jean Comaroff and
   John L. Comaroff, "Millennial Capitalism: First Thoughts on a Second Coming," pp.
   291–343. See also George F. DeMartino, *Global Economy, Global Justice: Theoretical
   Objections and Policy Alternatives to Neoliberalism* (New York and London: Routledge, 2000); Noam Chomsky, *Profit Over People: Neoliberalism and Global Order*
   (New York: Seven Stories Press, 1999); Andriana Vlachou, editor, *Contemporary Economic Theory: Radical Critiques of Neoliberalism* (New York: St. Martin's Press, 1999).

8. For especially nuanced accounts of the cultural politics of neoliberalism in the Latin
   American context, see the introduction and essays in Jacquelyn Chase, *The Spaces
   of Neoliberalism: Land, Place and Family in Latin America* (Bloomfield, Conn.: Krimarian Press, 2002).

9. See Judith Goode and Jeff Maskovsky, editors, *The New Poverty Studies: The Ethnography of Power, Politics, and Impoverished People in the United States* (New York: New
   York University Press, 2001). The introduction and essays collected in this volume
   trace the broad effects of neoliberal policies on poverty rates and the experience of
   impoverishment in the U.S., including examination of welfare and criminal justice
   and incarceration policies.

10. Lawrence Meade, *Beyond Entitlement: The Social Obligations of Citizenship* (New
    York: Free Press, 1986), pp. 84–85, quoted in Christian Parenti, *Lockdown America:
    Police and Prisons in the Age of Crisis* (New York and London: Verso, 1999), p. 168.

11. Anna Marie Smith, "The Sexual Regulation Dimension of Contemporary Welfare
    Law: A Fifty State Overview," *Michigan Journal of Gender and Law* 8, no. 2 (2002),
    pp. 121–218. Smith provides both an analysis of the 1996 reform and a brief summary
    of the history of welfare legislation in the United States, as well as an extensive list of
    citations for historical and legal studies of the welfare state.

12. Angela Davis, *The Prison Industrial Complex* (San Francisco: AK Press Audio Recording, 1997); Parenti, pp. 3–66. See also Sasha Abramsky, *Hard Time Blues: How Politics Built a Prison Nation* (New York: Thomas Dunne Books/St. Martin's Press, 2002).

13. Quoted in Parenti, p. 3.

14. Dick Armey, "Creating a World of Free Men," in David Boaz, editor, *Toward Liberty: The Idea That Is Changing the World* (Washington, D.C.: The Cato Institute, 2002), p. 428.

15. See for instance Stiglitz, Phillips, and "The Wickedness of Wall Street," *The Economist*, 8 June 2002, pp. 11–12.

Chapter 2, The Incredible Shrinking Public

1. See Carole Vance, editor, *Pleasure and Danger: Exploring Female Sexuality* (Boston: Routledge, 1984). This volume includes papers presented at the 1982 conference.

2. For a chronology and description of the sex wars debates, see Lisa Duggan and Nan Hunter, *Sex Wars: Sexual Dissent and Political Culture* (New York: Routledge, 1995).

3. See Cathy Cohen, *The Boundaries of Blackness: AIDS and the Breakdown of Black Politics* (Chicago, Ill.: University of Chicago Press, 1999) and Richard Meyer, *Outlaw Representation: Censorship and Homosexuality in Twentieth-Century American Art* (New York: Oxford University Press, 2002), for accounts of aspects of the AIDS and arts censorship debates.

4. The CBS *60 Minutes* segment aired on March 22, 1998.

5. Truth in Politics identified no other members in addition to Shipley. TIP had complained frequently in previous years about women's studies events, to little avail, though Shipley did join in the successful opposition to Rosemary Curb, a former nun, a lesbian, and a 1997 finalist for a deanship at SUNY New Paltz. In addition to the activity of TIP, some local observers noted that many figures involved in the attack on the "Revolting Behavior" conference had ties to the secretive, conservative Catholic organization, Opus Dei.

6. The friendly gay paper, the *New York Blade News,* 14 November 1997, pp. 1, 8, described the School of Fine and Performing Arts conference as including an art exhibit with enlarged photographs of vaginas and enlarged illustrations of female genitalia from *Gray's Anatomy,* a play about AIDS, and a seminar on the sexual content of Andy Warhol films.

7. The conference budget of $5,566 included $400 each from the Office of the President and the Office of the Dean of Arts & Sciences. The rest of the funds were from private sources and registration fees.

8. Bradford P. Wilson, "Politicizing Academic Freedom, Vulgarizing Scholarly Discourse," *Chronicle of Higher Education,* 19 December 1997.

9. "Panel Backs SUNY Campus on Sex Conference," *New York Times,* 23 December 1997, B5.

10. "A $350,000 Gift for SUNY," *New York Times*, 12 December 1997, A56.

11. For instance, The Center for Lesbian and Gay Studies at the CUNY Graduate Center defended the conference on both fronts, as did the New Caucus of the CUNY faculty union. A SUNY Stony Brook student newspaper editorial noted that de Russy's "opinions and initiatives would have even the Church Lady begging her to chill the fuck out."

12. Ryan's remarks were widely reported, including in the *New York Times* on 28 January 1998. De Russy's radio address was quoted in a 30 January 1998 National Coalition for Sexual Freedom press release.

13. "SUNY New Paltz braces for new round of criticism," *Albany Times Union*, 24 February 1998.

14. Alisa Solomon, "Sexual Smokescreen," *Village Voice*, 25 November 1997, p. 56.

15. For a discussion of Mario Cuomo's three terms and his move rightward under severe pressure from business and financial interests, see Sidney Plotkin and William E. Scheuerman, *Private Interest, Public Spending: Balanced Budget Conservatism and the Fiscal Crisis* (Boston: South End Press, 1994), Part 2, "A Case Study of New York."

16. My thanks to Liz Sevcenko who allowed me to cull information from her unpublished research paper, "Candace Camera: How Attacks on Queer Theory Support Conservative Politics."

17. Alisa Solomon, "Enemies of Public Education: Who Is Behind the Attacks on CUNY and SUNY?" *Village Voice Education Supplement*, 21 April 1998, pp. 2–4.

18. De Russy's memorandum is reprinted in Lorna Tychostup, "Chill Factor at SUNY New Paltz," *Chronogram*, November, 1999, p. 7.

19. Bowen provided a copy of this speech during a personal interview. He later published a much tamer version of this speech—see Roger Bowen, "The New Battle Between Political and Academic Cultures," *Chronicle of Higher Education*, 22 June 2001, B14–15. Bowen left SUNY to become president of the Public Museum in Milwaukee.

20. Quoted in Solomon, "Sexual Smokescreen."

21. For a discussion of similar conditions and events in California and Virginia during the mid- to late-1990s, see Annette Fuentes, "Trustees of the Right's Agenda," *The Nation*, 5 October 1998, pp. 19–21.

22. For accounts of various aspects of the "new conservatism" in the post-1970s U.S., see Amy Ansell, editor, *Unraveling the Right: The New Conservatism in American Thought and Politics* (Boulder, Colo.: Westview Press, 1998).

23. Clarence Y. H. Lo, *Small Property versus Big Government: Social Origins of the Property Tax Revolt* (Berkeley: University of California Press, 1990).

24. Thomas Byrne Edsall and Mary D. Edsall, *Chain Reaction: The Impact of Race, Rights and Taxes on American Politics* (New York: W. W. Norton & Co., 1991) makes the argument that race, rights, and taxes drove most U.S. politics 1965–1990.

25. For a definitive analysis of the racist impact of federal housing policy in the post–World War II period, see George Lipsitz, *The Possessive Investment in White-*

ness: How White People Profit from Identity Politics (Philadelphia, Pa.: Temple University Press, 1998).

26. Jean Stefancic and Richard Delgado, *No Mercy: How Conservative Think Tanks and Foundations Changed America's Social Agenda* (Philadelphia, Pa.: Temple University Press, 1996).

27. See the discussion of welfare politics in chapter 1.

28. These were Lynne Cheney's "gang of four," on her hit list during her tenure as chair of the National Endowment for the Humanities.

29. See Gary Rhoades and Sheila Slaughter, "Academic Capitalism, Managed Professionals and Supply-Side Education," and Bart Meyers, "The CUNY Wars," in *Social Text* 51 (summer 1997), pp. 9–38, 119–130. See also Neil Smith, "Giuliani Time: The Revanchist 1990s," *Social Text* 57 (winter 1998), pp. 1–20, especially pp. 14–15.

Chapter 3, Equality, Inc.

1. A transcript of Falwell's September 13 statement and responses to it were released by the National Lesbian and Gay Task Force. These and other post-9/11 events were reported by QueerMail@aol.com on September 14, 2001.

2. Bill Ghent, "Tragedy Changed Gay Climate," *National Journal*, 12 January 2002, p. 104.

3. See Suzanna Walters, *All the Rage: the Story of Gay Visibility in America* (Chicago, Ill.: University of Chicago Press, 2001).

4. The Clinton administration was the most inclusive of racial minorities and women of any presidential administration in U.S. history, though this inclusiveness did not lead to full equality of influence in the daily life of the administration. Cabinet departments led by women, including Donna Shalala's Health and Human Services and Janet Reno's Justice Department, tended to be marginalized; high level African-American appointees—for example, Joycelyn Elders's aborted tenure as Surgeon General and the failed nomination of Lani Guinier to the Civil Rights Division of the Justice Department—were likely to be treated as expendable window dressing. The Clinton administration's effort to eliminate the exclusion of lesbian and gay service members from the military, another historic effort, ended with an inadequate, ineffective, compromise policy. But the Bush administration's "diversity" has been far more limited, tokenistic, and cosmetic.

5. See Angela Dillard, *Who's Coming to Dinner Now? Multicultural Conservatism in America* (New York: New York University Press, 2001). For an example of "equality feminism," see the Independent Women's Forum Web site: www.iwf.org.

6. For a discussion of this attack on the New Deal coalition, and the central deployment of racism, see George Lipsitz, *American Studies in a Moment of Danger* (Minneapolis: University of Minnesota Press, 2001), chapter 4, pp. 83–114. For advocacy of this strategy, see Kevin Phillips, *The Emerging Republican Majority* (New Rochelle, N.Y.: Arlington House, 1969).

7. Not all national gay civil rights groups fall into the neoliberal camp—though most do. The National Gay and Lesbian Task Force (NGLTF) retains its progressive vision, as do some organizations representing racial, gender, or other sexual minorities (such as transgender groups).

8. Current HRC corporate sponsors include the right-wing, family-owned Coors Brewing Company, and Nike, a corporation often criticized and boycotted for its exploitative labor practices.

9. National Coalition of Anti-Violence Programs (NCAVP) press release, October 13, 2001.

10. Quoted in an email message from Michael Bronski, October 13, 2001.

11. Quoted in "'Liberty for All' Conference Spotlights Political Transformation Under Way in Gay Movement," Log Cabin Republican press release, August 30, 1999. The kind of superficial inclusiveness that characterized this conference, coupled with a harshly elitist agenda, received national attention during the August 2000 Republican Convention at which George W. Bush's "compassionate conservativism" was deceptively and manipulatively sold on network television.

12. http://www.indegayforum.org.

13. Richard Goldstein, *The Attack Queers: Liberal Society and the Gay Right* (London and New York: Verso, 2002).

14. Michael Warner, "Media Gays: A New Stone Wall," *The Nation*, 14 July 1997. Warner's article takes aim at a slightly different, though overlapping target than the neoliberal writers I examine here. He analyzes the conservative sexual politics of a broader group including many who would not fall under the neoliberal rubric—including for instance Larry Kramer, Gabriel Rotello, and Michelangelo Signorile, none of whom would be included in the IGF's new gay paradigm.

15. I am riffing here on the term *heteronormativity*, introduced by Michael Warner. I don't mean the terms to be parallel; there is no structure for gay life, no matter how conservative or normalizing, that might compare with the institutions promoting and sustaining heterosexual coupling.

16. I use "gay" throughout my discussion here, because this is the operative term for the neoliberals. Though they occasionally gesture toward lesbian inclusion, women and gender issues are not substantively addressed in any of their policy recommendations. Terms such as *bisexual, transgender,* or *queer* occur only as targets of ridicule. And, the presumptive whiteness of the audiences for these writers is unwavering.

17. The best description and analysis of the politics of the homophile movement remains John D'Emilio's classic *Sexual Politics, Sexual Communities: The Making of a Homosexual Minority in the United States, 1940–1970* (Chicago, Ill.: University of Chicago Press, 1983).

18. See John D'Emilio, *Sexual Politics*; Rodger Streitmatter, *Unspeakable: The Rise of the Lesbian and Gay Rights Press in America* (Boston: Faber & Faber, 1995); Jim Kepner, *Rough News—Daring Views: 1950s Pioneer Gay Press Journalism* (New York: The Haworth Press, 1998); and Manuela Soares, "The Purloined *Ladder*: Its Place in Les-

bian History," in Sonya Jones, ed., *Gay and Lesbian Literature Since World War II: History and Memory* (New York: The Haworth Press, 1998), pp. 27–49.

19. For an extended analysis of the 1980s antigay initiatives and the explosion of new queer activism in the face of AIDS, see Lisa Duggan and Nan Hunter, editors, *Sex Wars: Sexual Dissent and Political Culture* (New York: Routledge, 1995).

20. For a sharp analysis of this new gay moralism, see Michael Warner, *The Trouble with Normal: Sex, Politics and the Ethics of Queer Life* (New York: The Free Press, 1999).

21. Bruce Bawer, editor, *Beyond Queer: Challenging Gay Left Orthodoxy* (New York: The Free Press, 1996), introduction, pp. ix–xv, for "most gay people," "queerthink," and "postideological." For "silent majority" see his *A Place at the Table: The Gay Individual in American Society* (New York: Simon and Schuster, 1993), p. 26. The reference to "anachronistic" Stonewall politics is in his "Notes on Stonewall: Is the Gay Rights Movement Living in the Past?" *The New Republic*, 13 June 1994, p. 24.

22. Bruce Bawer, "Up (with) the Establishment," *The Advocate*, 23 January 1996, p. 112. The accusation of ideological extremism is from Bawer's review of Vaid's book, *Virtual Equality: The Mainstreaming of Gay and Lesbian Liberation* (New York: Doubleday, 1995), which appeared as "Radically Different: Do Gay People Have a Responsibility to be Revolutionaries?" in the *New York Times Book Review*, 5 November 1995, p. 21.

23. The text of this letter, published in *New York Times*, 11 September 1997, is included on a Web site with many other documents relating to this arts funding conflict, at http://hotx.com/esperanza/litigation. For an excellent brief summary of events, see Alexandra Chasin, *Selling Out: The Gay and Lesbian Movement Goes to Market* (New York: St. Martin's Press, 2000), pp. 228–233. The Esperanza Center has undergone repeated battles over the funding issue since 1997 and is still involved in litigation as of this writing.

24. Andrew Sullivan, *Virtually Normal: An Argument About Homosexuality* (New York: Alfred A. Knopf, 1995), p. 21.

25. Sullivan, *Virtually Normal*, p. 47.

26. Sullivan, *Virtually Normal*, pp. 69, 71. Sullivan cites U.S. social historian George Chauncey, historian and classicist David Halperin, and historical sociologist David Greenberg, so he cannot be unaware of the consensus against him on this point. He names only John Boswell, a medieval Catholic Church historian and nearly lone voice on the issue of unvarying homosexual identity, as support for his version of "history itself."

27. See Lisa Duggan, "Making It Perfectly Queer," in Duggan and Nan D. Hunter, *Sex Wars: Sexual Dissent and Political Culture* (New York: Routledge, 1995), pp. 155–172. This essay discusses both "outing" and the uses of "queer" in 1990s political debates.

28. Sullivan, *Virtually Normal*, pp. 85, 93.

29. Judith Butler, *Excitable Speech: A Politics of the Performative* (New York: Routledge, 1997).

30. For a restrained but scathing review of Sullivan's historical account in *Virtually*

Normal, see K. Anthony Appiah, "The Marrying Kind," *New York Review of Books,* 20 June 1996, pp. 48–52.

31. Sullivan, *Virtually Normal,* p. 151.

32. Sullivan, *Virtually Normal,* pp. 176–179.

33. Sullivan, *Virtually Normal,* p. 182.

34. Sullivan, *Virtually Normal,* p. 192. In a hilarious critique of gay conservative idealizations of marriage, "Gay Marriage? Don't Say I Didn't Warn You," *The Nation,* 29 April 1996, p. 9, Katha Pollitt writes,

> When gay friends argue in favor of same-sex marriage, I always agree and offer them the one my husband and I are leaving. Why should straights be the only ones to have their unenforceable promise to love, honor and cherish trap them like houseflies in the web of law? Marriage will not only open up to gay men and lesbians whole new vistas of guilt, frustration, claustrophobia, bewilderment, declining self-esteem, unfairness and sorrow, it will offer them the opportunity to prolong this misery by tormenting each other in court.

35. Sullivan, *Virtually Normal,* pp. 186–187.

36. In the epilogue to *Virtually Normal,* Sullivan indulges a strange ambivalence, acknowledging that gay life—always and only white gay male life—contains, in its differences, resources for the society at large. (His subject and audience are only ever presumptively white and male. For a perceptive exposure of the whiteness of Sullivan's "gays" see "Gay Male Identities, Personal Privacy, and Relations of Public Exchange: Notes on Directions for Queer Critique." In *Queer Transexions of Race, Nation, and Gender,* eds. Phillip Brian Harper, Anne McClintock, José Esteban Muñoz, and Trish Rosen. Special issue of *Social Text* 52/53 ([15.3–4; Fall/Winter 1997]: 5–29.) He points to the supportive role of friendship networks and to the admiral flexibility of many gay men who allow for "extramarital outlets" in their relationships. He was excoriated on the right for the "extramarital outlets" reference and retracted it in a new afterward to the paperback edition of the book. In a letter to the editor in *Commentary* (November 1996)—a response to an attack by Norman Podhoretz on this issue—Sullivan clarified that "It is my view that, in same-sex marriage, adultery should be as anathema as it is in heterosexual marriage." Well, one might ask, exactly how anathema is that?

37. AndrewSullivan.com, Daily Dish, September 23, 2001.

38. The New York Public Library flyer advertising Sullivan's lecture, "The Emasculation of Gay Politics," commented: "Mr. Sullivan will present his case for how the gay community went from defending sexual freedom to joining the victimology bandwagon: New Left feminism changed forever a kind of gay politics, and gay men are becoming alienated from their ostensible political institutions as a result." Elsewhere in his lectures and writings, Sullivan supported George W. Bush's presidency, the bombing of Afghanistan, and the war against Iraq, always with his flair for left-bashing. In "Did It Have to Be a Perfect Morning?" published in *The Times* of London on 15 September 2002, he wrote, "The middle part of the country—the great red zone

that voted for Bush—is clearly ready for war. The decadent Left in its enclaves on the coasts is not dead—and may well mount what amounts to a fifth column."

39. See the Liberty Education Forum Web site: www.libertyeducationforum.org.

40. An excellent discussion of the politics of right-wing libertarianism, including the activities of the Independent Women's Forum, is included in Jean Hardisty, *Mobilizing Resentment: Conservative Resurgence from the John Birch Society to the Promise Keepers* (Boston: Beacon Press, 1999), Chapter 6, "Libertarianism and Civil Society: The Romance of Free-Market Capitalism," pp. 162–188.

41. David Boaz, "Reviving the Inner City," in David Boaz and Edward Crane, editors, *Market Liberalism*, pp. 189–203. Boaz expounds his position on marriage vs. domestic partnership for gays in "Domestic Justice," *New York Times*, 4 January 1995.

Chapter 4, Love *and* Money

1. See Rosalind P. Petchesky, *Abortion and Woman's Choice: The State, Sexuality, and Reproductive Freedom* (Boston: Northeastern University Press, 1990).

2. See Luke W. Cole and Sheila R. Foster, *From the Ground Up: Environmental Racism and the Rise of the Environmental Justice Movement* (New York: New York University Press, 2000).

3. See any of a long list of publications by Cindy Patton, including *Inventing AIDS* (New York: Routledge, 1990), *Last Served? Gendering the HIV Pandemic* (New York: Taylor and Francis, 1994), and *Globalizing AIDS* (Minneapolis: University of Minnesota Press, 2002).

4. See Alexander Cockburn, Jeffrey St. Clair, and Allan Sekula, *Five Days That Shook the World: The Battle for Seattle and Beyond* (New York and London: Verso, 2001).

5. Internet Web sites circulated a vast range of political commentary following 9/11, through the war with Iraq and after, much faster and more inclusively than print publications. See, for example, the archive on www.counterpunch.com.

6. Coverage of the array of government measures and new legislation designed to fight "terrorism" by constricting civil liberties, for instance in the USA Patriot Act enacted following 9/11, was included in *The Nation* throughout the years, including the period during and after the 2003 war in Iraq.

7. See Alisa Solomon, "Which Third Way? Greens and the WFP Try to Make Progressive Votes Count," the *Village Voice*, 30 October 2000, 5 November 2000. Solomon argues that,

> The WFP, created in 1998 and built around progressive unions like the Communications Workers of America and grassroots advocacy groups like ACORN, exploits New York's allowance of "fusion"—which permits different parties to cross-endorse the same candidates. At this early stage, the WFP hardly ever puts forward its own candidates, but endorses Democrats in an effort to hold them accountable to the progressive ideals the WFP stands for. Among them: living wages, affordable housing, investment in schools. When asked, WFP will avow

support for gay rights and reproductive freedom, but you have to search long to learn that on the WFP Web site; economic justice is the party's essential cause.

8. Ralph Nader, *Crashing the Party: Taking on Corporate Government in an Age of Surrender* (New York: Thomas Dunne Books/St. Martin's Press, 2002). A discussion of *Roe v. Wade*, and feminist challenges to his position and statements, appear on pp. 261–267. There is no mention of the "gonadal politics" remark. This quote was reported widely on LGBT listserves and Web sites, but I have not been able to confirm it.

9. Nader, *Crashing the Party*, p. 103.

10. See Elizabeth "Betita" Martinez, "Where Was the Color in Seattle?" in Mike Prokosch and Laura Raymond, *The Global Activists Manual: Local Ways to Change the World* (New York: Thunder's Mouth Press/Nation Books, 2002), pp. 80–85.

11. Naomi Klein, *No Logo: No Space, No Choice, No Jobs* (New York: Picador USA, 2000), p. 122.

12. Thomas Frank, *One Market Under God: Extreme Capitalism, Market Populism, and the End of Economic Democracy* (New York: Anchor Books/Random House, Inc., 2000).

13. Todd Gitlin, *The Twilight of Common Dreams: Why America Is Wracked by Culture Wars* (New York: Henry Holt and Company, Inc., 1995).

14. Richard Rorty, *Achieving Our Country: Leftist Thought in Twentieth-Century America* (Cambridge: Harvard University Press, 1998).

15. Michael Tomasky, *Left for Dead: The Life, Death and Possible Resurrection of Progressive Politics in America* (New York: The Free Press, 1996), p. 25.

16. Wendy Brown, *States of Injury: Power and Freedom in Late Modernity* (Princeton, N.J.: Princeton University Press, 1995), especially Chapter 3: "Wounded Attachments," pp. 52–76. For examples of Cindy Patton's work, see footnote no. 3 above.

17. Wendy Brown, "Moralism as Antipolitics," in Russ Castronovo and Dana D. Nelson, editors, *Materializing Democracy: Toward a Revitalized Cultural Politics* (Durham and London: Duke University Press, 2002), p. 370.

18. Robin D. G. Kelley, *Freedom Dreams: The Black Radical Imagination* (Boston: Beacon Press, 2002).

19. Mary Poovey, "The Abortion Question and the Death of Man," in Judith Butler and Joan W. Scott, editors, *Feminists Theorize the Political* (New York and London: Routledge, 1992), pp. 239–256. Poovey intends to bring the insights of poststructuralism to the abortion controversy and to use them to complicate the "rights" claims structuring efforts to legalize abortion. She begins with the hope/expectation that her insights and suggestions will be controversial. But what Poovey seems not to realize, at all, is that the political implications of her critique were and are laughably, if not bitterly, obvious to seasoned reproductive freedom activists—especially those whose roots were in R2N2—Reproduction Rights National Network.

20. Nancy Fraser, *Justice Interruptus: Critical Reflections on the "Postsocialist" Condition*

(New York and London: Routledge, 1997). See also Fraser's "Rethinking Recognition," *New Left Review* 3 (May–June 2000).

21. Judith Butler, "Merely Cultural," and Nancy Fraser, "Heterosexism, Misrecognition, and Capitalism: A Response to Judith Butler," *Social Text* nos. 52–53 (Fall/Winter 1997), pp. 265–289. For a wide range of queer analyses with a central political economic component, see the work of Gayle Rubin, Cathy Cohen, Lauren Berlant, José Muñoz, Gayatri Gopinath, Nayan Shah, John Howard, and many others. Fraser appears to be unfamiliar with this literature.

22. Paul Gilroy, *Against Race: Imagining Political Culture Beyond the Color Line* (Cambridge: Harvard University Press, 2000).

23. Gilroy, *Against Race*, p. 262–263. For Wahneema Lubiano's approach, see her "Black Nationalism and Black Common Sense: Policing Ourselves and Others," in Wahneema Lubiano, editor, *The House That Race Built* (New York: Vintage, 1998), pp. 232–252.

24. Robin D. G. Kelley, *Yo' Mama's Disfunktional! Fighting the Culture Wars in Urban America* (Boston: Beacon Press, 1997), and Kelley, *Freedom Dreams*.

25. Eric Lott, "After Identity, Politics," *New Literary History* special issue: "Is There Life After Identity Politics?" 31, no. 4 (Autumn 2000), p. 666. See also his "Boomer Liberalism," *Transition* 78 (1999); "The New Cosmopolitanism," *Transition* 72 (1997); and "New Black Intellectuals," *Transition* 68 (1995).

26. Amber Hollibaugh and Nikhil Pal Singh, "Sexuality, Labor, and the New Trade Unionism: A Conversation," in Kitty Krupat and Patrick McCreery, editors, *Out at Work: Building a Gay-Labor Coalition* (Minneapolis: University of Minnesota Press, 2001), pp. 60–77. See also Krupat's "Out of Labor's Dark Ages: Sexual Politics Comes to the Workplace," pp. 1–23 of the same volume.

Selected Bibliography

Abramsky, Sasha. *Hard Time Blues: How Politics Built a Prison Nation.* New York: Thomas Dunne Books/St. Martin's Press, 2002.

Ansell, Amy, editor. *Unraveling the Right: The New Conservatism in American Thought and Politics.* Boulder, Colo.: Westview Press, 1998.

Bawer, Bruce. *A Place at the Table: The Gay Individual in American Society.* New York: Simon and Schuster, 1993.

———. *Beyond Queer: Challenging Gay Left Orthodoxy.* New York: The Free Press, 1996.

Boaz, David. *Toward Liberty: The Idea That Is Changing the World.* Washington, D.C.: The Cato Institute, 2002.

Brown, Wendy. *States of Injury.* Princeton, N.J.: Princeton University Press, 1995.

Chase, Jacquelyn. *The Spaces of Neoliberalism: Land, Place and Family in Latin America.* Bloomfield, Conn.: Krimarian Press, 2002.

Chasin, Alexandra. *Selling Out: the Gay and Lesbian Movement Goes to Market.* New York: St. Martin's Press, 2000.

Chomsky, Noam. *Profit Over People: Neoliberalism and Global Order.* New York: Seven Stories Press, 1999.

Cockburn, Alexander, Jeffrey St. Clair, and Allan Sekula. *Five Days That Shook the World: The Battle for Seattle and Beyond.* New York and London: Verso, 2001.

Cohen, Cathy. *The Boundaries of Blackness: AIDS and the Breakdown of Black Politics.* Chicago, Ill.: University of Chicago Press, 1999.

Cole, Luke W., and Sheila R. Foster. *From the Ground Up: Environmental Racism and the Rise of the Environmental Justice Movement.* New York: New York University Press, 2000.

Davis, Angela. *The Prison Industrial Complex.* San Francisco, Calif.: AK Press Audio Recording, 1997.

DeMartino, George F. *Global Economy, Global Justice: Theoretical Objections and Policy Alternatives to Neoliberalism.* New York and London: Routledge, 2000.

D'Emilio, John. *Sexual Politics, Sexual Communities: The Making of a Homosexual Minority in the United States, 1940–1970.* Chicago, Ill.: University of Chicago Press, 1983.

Dillard, Angela. *Who's Coming to Dinner Now? Multicultural Conservatism in America.* New York: New York University Press, 2001.

Duggan, Lisa, and Nan D. Hunter. *Sex Wars: Sexual Dissent and Political Culture.* New York: Routledge, 1995.

Edsall, Thomas Byrne, and Mary D. Edsall. *Chain Reaction: Race, Rights and Taxes in American Politics.* New York: W. W. Norton & Co., 1991.

Fraser, Nancy. *Justice Interruptus: Critical Reflections on the "Postsocialist" Condition*. New York and London: Routledge, 1997.

Gilroy, Paul. *Against Race: Imagining Political Culture Beyond the Color Line*. Cambridge, Mass.: Harvard University Press, 2000.

Goldstein, Richard. *The Attack Queers: Liberal Society and Gay Rights*. London and New York: Verso, 2002.

Goode, Judith, and Jeff Maskovsky, editors. *The New Poverty Studies: The Ethnography of Power, Politics, and Impoverished People in the United States*. New York: New York University Press, 2001.

Hardisty, Jean. *Mobilizing Resentment: Conservative Resurgence from the John Birch Society to the Promise Keepers*. Boston: Beacon Press, 1999.

Kelley, Robin D. G. *Freedom Dreams: The Black Radical Imagination*. Boston: Beacon Press, 2002.

———. *Yo' Mama's Disfunktional! Fighting the Cutlure Wars in Urban America*. Boston: Beacon Press, 1997.

Krupat, Kitty, and Patrick McCreery, editors. *Out at Work: Building a Gay-Labor Coalition*. Minneapolis: University of Minnesota Press, 2001.

Lipsitz, George. *The Possessive Investment in Whiteness: How White People Profit from Identity Politics*. Philadelphia, Pa.: Temple University Press, 1998.

———. *American Studies in a Moment of Danger*. Minneapolis: University of Minnesota Press, 2001.

Lloyd, David, and Paul Thomas. *Culture and the State*. New York and London: Routledge, 1998.

Lo, Clarence. *Small Property versus Big Government: Social Origins of the Property Tax Revolt*. Berkeley: University of California Press, 1990.

Lott, Eric. "After Identity, Politics." *New Literary History*, special issue: "Is There Life After Identity Politics?" 31, 4 (2000).

McHugh, Kathleen. *American Domesticity*. New York: Oxford University Press, 1999.

Meyer, Richard. *Outlaw Representation: Censorship and Homosexuality in Twentieth-Century American Art*. New York: Oxford University Press, 2002.

Parenti, Christian. *Lockdown America: Police and Prisons in the Age of Crisis*. New York and London: Verso, 1999.

Patton, Cindy. *Inventing AIDS*. New York: Routledge, 1990.

———. *Last Served? Gendering the HIV Pandemic*. New York: Taylor and Francis, 1994.

———. *Globalizing AIDS*. Minneapolis: University of Minnesota Press, 2002.

Petchesky, Rosalind P. *Abortion and Woman's Choice: The State, Sexuality, and Reproductive Freedom*. Boston: Northeastern University Press, 1990.

Peters, Michael. *Poststructuralism, Marxism and Neoliberalism*. New York: Rowman, Littlefield Publishers, Inc., 2001.

Phillips, Kevin. *The Emerging Republican Majority*. New Rochelle, N.Y.: Arlington House, 1969.

———. *Wealth and Democracy: A Political History of the American Rich*. New York: Broadway Books, 2002.

Polanyi, Karl. *The Great Transformation.* Boston: Beacon, 1944.

Smith, Anna Marie. "The Sexual Regulation Dimension of Contemporary Welfare Law: A Fifty State Overview." *Michigan Journal of Gender and Law* 8, 2 (2002): 121–218.

Stefancic, Jean, and Richard Delgado. *No Mercy: How Conservative Think Tanks and Foundations Changed America's Social Agenda.* Philadelphia, Pa.: Temple University Press, 1996.

Steinmetz, George, editor. *State/Culture: State-Formation after the Cultural Turn.* Ithaca and London: Cornell University Press, 1999.

Stiglitz, Joseph. *Globalization and Its Discontents.* New York and London: W. W. Norton, 2002.

Sullivan, Andrew. *Virtually Normal.* New York: Alfred A. Knopf, 1995.

Vaid, Urvashi. *Virtual Equality: The Mainstreaming of Gay and Lesbian Liberation.* New York: Doubleday, 1995.

Vlachou, Andriana, editor. *Contemporary Economic Theory: Radical Critiques of Neoliberalism.* New York: St. Martin's Press, 1999.

Walters, Suzanna. *All the Rage: The Story of Gay Visibility in America.* Chicago, Ill.: University of Chicago Press, 2001.

Warner, Michael. *The Trouble with Normal: Sex, Politics and the Ethics of Queer Life.* New York: The Free Press, 1999.

Acknowledgments

Writing this book was not a choice; it demanded to be written, and I eventually complied. Living in the United States during the past thirty years has been such a wild ride, offering moments of dizzying hope along with long stretches of political depression. I have relied on a network of friends, allies, congenial colleagues, questing students, and fellow travelers to keep me grounded. So many of them in so many places helped me think about neoliberalism, sex, race, gender and class, identity politics, activism, history and the progressive-left that I can't hope to thank them all. But I want to begin by thanking Henry Abelove, Tricia Rose, Claire Potter, Judith Halberstam, and José Muñoz, who provided crucial support and lively challenges all through the process of thinking through and writing this book. Their presence constitutes the amazing grace my Catholic grade school teachers talked so much about.

Diligent and joyful research assistance for this book was provided by Alyosha Goldstein, Micol Siegel, and Liz Sevcenko. The Faculty Working Group in Queer Studies at NYU read various drafts, and I am especially grateful to Carolyn Dinshaw, José Muñoz, Ann Pellegrini, Janet Jakobsen, Phil Harper, Anna McCarthy, Licia Fiol-Matta, Robert Corber, Patty White, and Chris Straayer. My superduper colleague in American Studies, Arlene Davila, also read drafts and responded with characteristic sharp intelligence and generosity. The faculty fellows' seminar on Gender, Sexuality and Cultural Politics at Vanderbilt University was extraordinarily generous during my year there; I'd like to thank Carolyn Dever, John Sloop, Kathryn Schwarz, Lynn Enterline, Katie Crawford, Holly Tucker, Brooke Ackerly, José Medina, Diane Perpich, Chuck Morris, and Lynn Clarke. My work and happiness at Vanderbilt were also enhanced immeasurably by Mona Frederick and

Galyn Martin. My Public Feelings group, a subformation of the Feminism and Sexuality Project, contributed substantially to my thinking, writing, and general pleasure—they supplied many ideas about political depression, and how to survive it! Thanks especially to Deb Gould, Mary Patten, Ann Cvetkovich, Lauren Berlant, Sasha Torres, Ann Reynolds, and Neville Hoad.

Colleagues and audiences at various college and university lectures contributed questions and insights: Wesleyan University (Henry Abelove and Claire Potter), UC San Diego (Judith Halberstam), UC Riverside (Jennifer Doyle and Molly McGarry), UCLA (Sandra Harding), Duke University (Karen Krahulik and Robyn Wiegman), the University of Washington at Seattle (Chandan Reddy and Brandy Paris), University of Miami (Russ Castronovo), Barnard College (Janet Jakobsen), George Mason University (Roger Lancaster) and Northwestern University (Tessie Liu). For exceptionally useful feedback on draft chapters or while I was on the road, I would also like to thank Cathy Cohen, Judith Stacey, Mandy Merck, Dana Nelson, Ann Cvetkovich, Nan Hunter, Laura Kipnis, Michael Warner, David Halperin, Valerie Traub, Cora Kaplan, Beth Povinelli, Amy Kesselman (who provided crucial research access for chapter 2), and Roger Bowen (who graciously agreed to speak with me).

There is no adequate way to convey how grateful I am to my editor at Beacon, Amy Caldwell, whose patience and dogged support made all the difference in my getting this project into print. In addition, for setting the highest standard in political reporting against which I can only hope to measure up, I'd like to thank Alisa Solomon—in my humble opinion, the best investigative journalist in the country.

Finally, I would like to thank four people who didn't have anything directly to do with this book but who nonetheless have been crucial to me while writing it. Andrew Ross has been the visionary Director of American Studies at NYU during my several lifetimes there. His leadership made this a uniquely engaged and enlivening location for writing, teaching, and progressive politics; working with him during the past decade has been the highlight of my professional life. Robin Kelley, my colleague in the NYU history department, has been a breathtaking model for activist intellectual practice and ethics; his generosity is legendary. Cindy Patton is the queer activist intellectual of my dreams, cited in that mode throughout this book, and I miss her. And finally, Chris Straayer has been with me in one way or another since I first discovered "queer studies," through her then unpublished dissertation, in 1990. She knows, I hope, what this has meant to me.

Index